**Finding Quiet in
the Swiss Alps:
A Journey**

LIVE
WILDLY

First published 2020
by Live Wildly Ltd

www.livewildly.co

Copyright
© Lucy Fuggle, 2020

Printed by
L.E.G.O SPA, Vicenza,
Italy

Map on endpapers
Reproduced with permission
of swisstopo

(BAT200041)

Cover design by
Alana Louise Lyons

Interior design by

Collette Sadler

**Pen and ink
illustrations by**
Louise Morgan

Photography by
Lucy Fuggle
unless specified
otherwise

ISBN 978-1-8381198-0-5

contents

WATCHING THE WORLD

THINGS FALL APART

REBUILDING

STABLE GROUND

" As long as I live, I'll hear waterfalls
and birds and winds sing. I'll interpret
the rocks, learn the language of flood,
storm, and the avalanche. I'll acquaint
myself with the glaciers and wild
gardens, and get as near the heart
of the world as I can. "

THE JOURNALS OF JOHN MUIR (1899)

THE VIEW FROM MY DINING ROOM OF THE DARK ROCKFACE
OF THE WELLHORN WITH THE WETTERHORN AND ROSENLAUI
GLACIER BEHIND. BELOW ARE THE REICHENBACH FALLS.

slowing down

As the previous tenant tells me when I come to view the house on one of the first warm days of May, the only people who visit Meiringen are climbers and Sherlock Holmes fans. Tucked away in a valley in the mountainous heart of central Switzerland, it's a town of less than five thousand people, the bulk of them farmers, mountain people and other sleepy village folk.

We stand by the bedroom window looking out at the jagged peaks of the Engelhörner mountain range that I'll soon fall in love with. The winter snow is stubbornly clinging to the rocks, but life is blooming below: the mountainside covered in a forest green interrupted only by the tumult of glacial meltwater rushing down the Reichenbach Falls towards the River Aare.

The middle-aged woman – an artist, judging by the apartment's spare room-turned-studio, who is moving back to Bern – points out the names of the other mountains that frame the view. I try to remember them: the Wetterhorn and the Wellhorn, with the Rosenlaui glacier between them.

She warns me not to expect nightlife and excitement. That suits me just fine. Climbers and Sherlock Holmes fans are my kind of people anyway.

1

WOOD

You catch the smell of wood as soon as you enter the house. It's sweet and heavy on your nose. It's no surprise, really: the place is made of timber. The walls and floor are local pinewood. The ceilings have thick wooden beams. The doors, with delicately carved corners and a sheer bulk that weighs down their hinges, are made of it too.

The house is a product of the forest that creeps up the sides of the valley. It's full of markings, imperfections and stories of its history.

Each piece of wood in the house shows a character and complex beauty that I look to on days when my confidence leaves me and I'm left staring at the ceiling and hoping that silent reassurance will appear from somewhere. The house is a perfectly orchestrated layering of years of growth, put together to make something beautiful, strong and warm.

Generations have lived here to lead up to this moment; my books on the shelf, my postcards decorating the walls and my coffee press on the kitchen dresser. For now, it's my home.

2
CHANGE

I can't say I came to Switzerland because I wanted to live deliberately, simply, or anything like that. I first came here for love – for Iain, a Scot I met in Bergen, the European capital of rainfall nestled between seven mountains in the west of Norway. After forty-eight hours in the same hostel, I knew I was going to visit him in Switzerland, where he was doing his PhD in Zurich. And after visiting him, I knew I would move here.

I adored Switzerland from the start – the unfathomably blue glacial lakes I didn't think really existed, the vastness of the mountains, even the rules and strictness of the German-speaking cantons where recycling glass at lunchtime is a reportable offence.

Although Iain was in Zurich, I first made my base further south. I found myself in Interlaken, a tourist hotspot two hours away by train and nestled between Lakes Thun and Brienz. I got a job as a writer at a small travel software company, and spent my first eight months living among Interlaken's crowds and sharing an apartment with two colleagues.

For most months of the year, and reaching an unbearable peak in summer, Interlaken is crammed with tourists. They don't hang around long, often just spending a day here before moving on to the next city: Lucerne yesterday and Milan tomorrow. But there's a constant crowd, especially on the high street I walked along on my way to and from work.

Tourists flock to the best viewpoint to take in one of Switzerland's most iconic mountains: the Jungfrau. The contours are by no means as striking as the Matterhorn in Zermatt – by comparison, it's decidedly flat – but it's big. It's imposing enough to make you stop, gaze and watch the clouds slide over the white of the glacier for a while. At the best photo spot, there's a fountain surrounded by beds of coordinating pansies that somehow remain undamaged by the many visitors striking absurd poses.

The Jungfrau is beautiful, but the thing about the Berner Oberland region is that everything is beautiful. Most towns here have mountain views and lakes nearby. Interlaken is just the one that everyone comes to. The Swiss probably secretly appreciate this – all the other quiet towns are left for them to enjoy.

Living in Interlaken, I knew I was in one of the most stunning parts of Switzerland: in the heartland of the Swiss Alps, with the Eiger, Mönch and Jungfrau towering over the alpine towns below. But things weren't right. I lose myself in crowds. I'm terrible at living with people. I need space and time and loneliness.

When I went to the kitchen to get a glass of water one evening, my housemates were drinking Slovenian cherry schnapps before heading out to the only club in Interlaken and they wanted me to join them. "Have one shot and we'll leave you alone, we promise," one of them said, pouring me a glass and knowing how much I love being left alone. I took the shot, and we exchanged the smiles that signal we both know what I'm like and that I'm not going to change. Then I went to bed.

I thought of all the other Swiss mountain towns just a few miles from Interlaken, many of which I had visited on weekends, and wanted their silence.

I wanted to live how I really wanted, even if that meant turning against what everyone I knew was doing. I didn't want to be close to the action or save on rent by sharing space anymore. I wanted to live somewhere with quiet views of the mountains, surrounded by nature and with plenty of time to sit, read, write and think.

I wanted to see the light change on the horizon, to notice the pinky-orange alpenglow illuminating the mountains as the day fell away and to know the comings and goings of the birds. I wanted to have places to explore and escape to. I wanted to live on my terms, no matter what people thought of that.

And I managed, somehow, to actually do it. While Iain stayed in Zurich, I made my own journey to Meiringen, just 30km from Interlaken but far enough for the droves of tourists to not bother visiting; to live alone next to the mountains and be surrounded by the waterfalls and hideouts of the birds.

In some ways I don't know how I ended up here, so far from the sheep farm in the south east of England I grew up on, wellington-booted and with a mass of unruly red curls. But then again, I do. It was all designed, one step at a time, even if there was no initial blueprint. I slowed down, listened and kept moving closer to where I wanted to be. And with faith, I got here.

MY DINING ROOM IN MEIRINGEN.

3
GOATS

When I first came to Meiringen to view the house, there was a goat market on the Casinoplatz in the town centre, close to the statue of Sherlock Holmes pondering something unknowable while holding his pipe. There were about a hundred goats, all lined up and ready for farmers to take their pick, drive them back to their mountain farms, and give them a new place to roam. I looked up at the contours of the unfamiliar mountain ranges on either side of the valley, the snowfall visible in May amongst spring's freshness.

There was not a single group of tourists in sight, and I suspected there weren't many women living alone here. I don't speak German, and I absolutely do not speak the farmers' dialect Swiss German that bounces impossibly between locals in conversation. But on that day, as the goats found their new pastures, I wondered if Meiringen's mountains would have me too.

4
LOVE

I spent less than forty-eight hours with Iain when I first met him in Bergen. On the first night of two, we chatted about Haruki Murakami and Radiohead and Scottish independence until one-thirty in the morning, when I realised I'd locked my key in my hostel room. I joked I could sneak into his all-male dorm just once before backing down and accepting my only option was the hostel sofa.

I slept terribly, if at all, and went to sheepishly find the receptionist when she arrived at seven to tell her my story in exchange for opening the door to my room. Showered and in clean clothes, I found Iain eating breakfast in the dining room and sat down to eat my cereal bar. He was going to take the train to Flåm, hire a bike to cycle to Geirangerfjord down a zigzagging mountainside overlooking waterfalls descending into the lake and take a boat trip from there. He invited me to join him.

Sleepy and self-conscious at the thought of embarrassing myself on a bike, I said no, and watched him trying to decipher my motives. I told him I hoped I'd see him later, and I meant it. As I wandered Bergen's art galleries, I asked myself why I didn't say yes to spending more time with this intriguing person I hardly knew before I had to leave the next day. Struggling to navigate the lands of flirtation, I went by the book: stay mysterious and unfazed, even if that's a lie of monstrous proportions.

I collected my thoughts on the artwork that I hoped to share with Iain later, then braved the drizzly weather to explore and pick up *Kanelsnurrer*, my favourite cinnamon buns woven with the effortless beauty shared between Scandinavian baking and their women's hairstyles.

Iain fascinated me: his intelligence about the books he'd read and his thoughts on the world. His type of Scottish accent I hadn't really heard before, with a lilt that he placed south-east of Glasgow. How I couldn't work out what he thought of me. How he was catching the Hurtigruten ferry up the Norwegian coastline before heading to Svalbard, the island above Russia on the upper tip of the Arctic. I had dreamt of visiting it too, despite not yet finding the courage to go on my own wild adventures. This trip was my first time even properly travelling alone.

That night I sat in the hostel's communal area with a book, *Out Stealing Horses* by Per Petterson, half reading and half keeping an eye on who was coming in and out. A couple of hours later, he found me and invited me for a walk around Bergen, through the town and down to the water's edge. This time, I said yes. I grabbed my obnoxiously yellow raincoat and we resumed our easy way of conversation as we walked away from the hostel, him talking about the fjords, me about the art I'd seen that day.

For two hours we wandered the town and got to know the corners of each other's lives. As night fell, we sat on a bench overlooking the city lights and our conversation dimmed to a pause. He looked at me and smiled, thinking something to himself. Eventually, he asked if he could kiss me. I put my hand on his shoulder and responded with my own smile, realising this could be something after all, just hours before we would head our separate ways.

When I left Bergen after breakfast the next morning, we kissed goodbye and exchanged contact details, sharing comments on each other's peculiar surnames. He explained his was Polish, inherited from his grandfather who had made his way to Scotland after the Second World War.

Two weeks after I got back to England following distracted wandering in Stockholm, Copenhagen and Berlin, as well as going to my university graduation ceremony in Devon, I came to visit Iain in Zurich.

5
SWITZERLAND

For two weeks, Iain gave me my first taste of Switzerland, the place he'd been getting to know for the past year, as well as during an earlier stint for an internship in Basel.

He was my tour guide as we ate *rösti* with fried egg in Zurich's old side streets and white wine fondue during a lakeside weekend in Italian-speaking Ticino. But he also pushed me to go off and explore further afield alone. He had to go back to work in his lab for a few days, and he assured me it'd be worth it.

I was quietly reluctant; I wanted to stay close to him for my two weeks in Switzerland and was already enjoying the familiarity of Zurich. But when he first met me in Norway, I was someone who travelled alone and sought out adventures – even if that was my first ever time doing so. I had his expectations to uphold, and I didn't want to let him down. I wanted to be the interesting and independent woman he thought I was, even if it still felt like an entirely alien role to me.

I booked train tickets across the country to Zermatt, spending the next two nights sleeping in a roasting-hot hostel room with strangers. By day, I had my first experience in the Swiss mountains, making do with the trainers I had with me in the absence of any hiking boots and wandering up to lakes with a view of the Matterhorn I recognised from Toblerone packets.

Packing up my little backpack with the bare essentials I had with me, I did what tourists do next and took the Glacier Express train across to St Moritz. The day-long journey drifted by with the backdrop of music Iain had recommended to me, "Hounds" by The Antlers, playing as the train burrowed through the mountains and exited to glide over waterfalls. They pulsed with so much elegant power, too fleeting for any photo but breathtaking enough to remember years later.

For my day in St Moritz, aware of how much I was bringing down the average age and wealth, I headed to the lake, drawn to the freely blooming wildflowers surrounding it. As I stopped for the lunch of bread and cheese I'd picked up at the supermarket, an older Dutch couple stopped me and insisted they take my photo next to the lake.

When I got back to Zurich that evening, I caught the bus to Iain's apartment and let myself in the door he'd left open for me. I found him in his kitchen, breathed him in as I hugged him and felt sure I was finding my home.

A month later, I knew what I'd do next. I packed a hand luggage bag and moved to Switzerland.

EXPLORING ST MORITZ ON MY FIRST TRIP TO SWITZERLAND.

" Meiringen is the chief place in the vale of Hasli, and an excellent specimen of a Swiss village. The picturesqueness of its situation, in the midst of a truly Alpine vale, is much praised. The precipitous and wooded mountain sides, streaked with cascades, and here and there overtopped by some snow-peak, are beautiful features. "

JOHN MURRAY, 1874

6

MOVING

I move my belongings from Interlaken to Meiringen on a warm evening in June, packing my books, bedding, clothes, orchid and a few pieces of kitchenware into my friend Stephen's car. The journey isn't long, only half an hour's drive from the apartment where I have spent the last eight months.

We drive out of Interlaken, already busy with summer tourists, and along the Brienzersee, the blue glacial lake to the eastern side of Interlaken. After reaching the end of the water, it's another few miles' drive through the farm country of the Haslital and along the grey-blue water of the River Aare. Soon enough, the tall *Kletterhalle*, the climbing gym, comes into sight, followed by the tennis courts and chilly outdoor pool fed with water straight from the Aare.

Meiringen, likely birthplace of the meringue, is a Swiss mountain town made for postcards. Most of the houses are built from timber, using traditional construction techniques and showing off overhanging roofs and window boxes stuffed with red and pink geraniums. My house is one of the oldest, with a rose shrub crawling up the front and a gnarled apple tree by the summer house in the garden. I'll be taking the top floor with views in every direction and a balcony looking over to the jagged peaks of the Gelmerhörner mountain range in the distance.

We park up and take a few minutes to unpack the car. The house is quiet, but warm evening light is flooding through the dining room windows and into the kitchen. As I open the windows, birdsong rushes in, and we look at the mountain range and listen to the waterfalls. It's a retreat from the world, and the fact it's going to be mine for the near future still seems crazy.

I won't be staying there tonight. I'm flying to Greeland, where I'll spend a few weeks wandering the Arctic under the disorienting midnight sun. For most of that time I'll be on the west coast, in Ilulissat, which means "icebergs" in the Kalaallisut language. The town is well-named: here towering masses of ice are the monuments spellbinding locals and tourists every day. It's my first trip to such a remote place alone, booked spontaneously with a firm feeling that I should do it without asking for a second opinion. Like all other good big decisions, I feel out of my comfort zone, a little nervous, and I'm counting down the hours until I arrive.

For now, I show Stephen around and imagine my life here out loud. We look out the windows and I try to point out the names of the mountains that I learnt on my first visit. We sit on the unusually bouncy sofa, which looks like a relic from the 1950s, and compare thoughts on whether it's a good or bad type of bounce. As we stand in my bathroom, looking out the window over my balcony and towards the Gelmerhörner mountain range, Stephen comments on how spectacular the view from my toilet is going to be.

Next to the back of the wood burner stove in the dining room, we notice an unusual metal pot, delicately engraved, circular and about 60cm wide with a lid slightly propped open by whatever's inside. "What's in there?" asks Stephen. I have no idea. We open it up and find three huge crystals, each several kilos heavy and coated in stubborn dust like everything else in the box. In the kitchen, I discover another relic: a spectacularly curved metal pipe that Bilbo Baggins would be proud of, embossed with tiny flowers and a cap with a small chain to keep it attached to its end.

I choose my favourite of the crystals, one with a perfectly smooth edge, and gently rinse it in the kitchen sink. The dust rubs off and a swirly pink surface reveals itself. I put it on the kitchen counter, wondering when it last saw sunlight.

"Won't you get lonely here?" Stephen asks. "I'm not sure," I respond.

Even though I need solitude, it's not always good for me. I have no idea how this decision will shape the course of the next few years. But whether or not it's going to be easy, it just feels right to be here.

I get into the car with Stephen and we head back to Interlaken. The next time I'll be here, I'll have just got back from above the Arctic Circle. Everything will be new, unfamiliar and unwritten. And this will be my home.

THE OLD YET FUNCTIONING WOOD BURNER IN MY KITCHEN.

7
WAKING UP

Waking up here on the first day after I return from Greenland, I have complete faith in my decision to do what few people I know would do: to live alone away from friends and family, in a town that doesn't speak my language, and build a quiet life in the shadow of mountains.

I open my eyes to the Engelhörner mountain range for the first time, the birds singing while swooping between their best-loved spots that I'd soon come to recognise. I'm in my hideaway in the Alps, a place I'd love to escape to for even a few days – and I've found a way to live here.

There's no phone line or internet yet, and there never has been. When the landlady asks me if I'd like the company to come and fit the cables, I pause for a few moments to imagine the bliss of a complete detox from the digital world. It's appealing, but I know it's not possible to stay completely disconnected. Only a couple of months into my job in Interlaken, I managed to negotiate working from home every Thursday and Friday. No one is really sure how I ended up with a privilege no one else in the company has, but now it's been so long that it's too late to question it. My unspoken end of the deal is to actually work on my home office days.

Before the house enters the future, I catch up on reading, head out on long walks and leave my phone in a drawer. When I need to work, I wander down to the Hotel Victoria in the town to use their wi-fi. It's warm and comfy in the café area of the hotel restaurant, with a relaxed vibe until dinner approaches and the formalities of venison and wine menus and tiny chocolate soufflés decorated with sugar-dusted raspberries arrive. The recurring presence of an elderly woman in the window seat doing crossword puzzles with a magnifying glass makes me feel better about being there so long. I make my green tea and complementary biscuit last as long as possible.

I explore the streets of my new town tentatively, realising how much of an outsider I must look. Unlike in Interlaken, most of the people I pass here acknowledge me with a smile and a greeting. The first few times this happens, I panic and just smile back, feeling unprepared and not knowing what they've said. The rich dialect here can be a struggle even for people in Interlaken to understand, let alone those from the cities. Some Swiss people claim that residents of the Berner Oberland can recognise the village a speaker is from by their dialect, and with the impressive vocal gymnastics around me on every trip to buy groceries or get the train to Interlaken, I'm not surprised. During Iain's first trip, I ask him what they're saying, and he has no clue either, even though he speaks comfortable German in Zurich.

I start responding with my best interpretation of the greetings I'm given: *morgä* in the mornings, *abä* in the evenings. It's obvious I'm not from around here, and it's not just my accent: I'm alone, shy away from conversations that would show my complete lack of the language and feel like an obnoxiously out-of-place foreign redhead. The locals don't seem to care too much, I'm always greeted by a smile and *Haslideutsch* nonetheless.

WAKING UP TO THE ENGELHÖRNER MOUNTAIN RANGE IN WINTER.

8

LONE WOLF

Being different is something I've long been used to, but I've not always had the guts to show it. As a kid I'd spend days sitting on my bedroom floor making things: magazines about the animals of the world, stories about magical dragons and designs of imaginary islands with all of the required infrastructure for a functioning society. I was shy but bright, and never had any problems at school other than keeping to myself and not raising my hand to ask or answer a single question during the course of my education.

I was perfectly happy with this existence, but the problems came in the next few years when I realised just how different I really was. As my body changed and signs of adulthood started surfacing, so did doubts about myself and whether I was good enough for the world around me.

I feared rejection more than anything. Every day became a challenge of fitting in and exchanging my ideas and weirdness for invisibility. The next few years were a confusing whirlwind of soaring self-doubt and, eventually, generalized and social anxiety disorders as well as what turned out to be post-traumatic stress. Stuck in the darkness, I physically and emotionally harmed myself for sucking so badly at this thing called life.

As soon as I heard about autism and what it can look like for women, things suddenly made more sense. By reading about others who were shining their own light and giving other people's expectations the finger, I saw a different path. I started having glimpses once more of the real me underneath it all, sitting on my bedroom floor bringing my ideas and voice into the world just as I was. I had lost sight of the joy that brought me. With all of the noise and buzz of other people's expectations and projections of how your life should be lived, the hardest thing can be to work out who you are and what you really want. I knew that was exactly what I needed to do.

I needed to get back to my dreams and imagination, and guard and fight for them with all I had. And at this moment, that meant moving to the mountains and carving out a life that no one else I knew could really understand.

Here in Meiringen, I feel more at peace than I have in eight months of living in Interlaken, even though I'm noticeably under the weather, perhaps from my few weeks of travelling. For the last few days, I've been in bed looking out the window and only getting up to make tea, admiring the view as the kettle boils.

I think I hear people knock on the door – my neighbours, probably – but, in my pyjamas and looking frightening, I never get up to answer. I never find the confidence to go over and properly introduce myself. We say hello as we pass each other while going about our days, but we all keep to ourselves. I'm more alone than I've ever been. But the thing is, I know I am recharging and slowly finding my way back to where I need to be. Back to myself.

9
WHY I CAME TO THE MOUNTAINS

I came to Meiringen to find a hideaway in the mountains. A place where I could live quietly, slow down, and make a nest for myself somewhere new. I was fed up with living with other people, the usual irritations of dishes in the sink, and having to make an excuse for being so quiet. I knew I wanted to live alone, so I searched within an hour of my work for places that were truly me. A place to watch the stars, read my books, listen to music, and pack a bag and flask of tea to go on adventures alone or with Iain when he visits on weekends.

I shortlisted two places: one was in Grindelwald, about forty minutes from my office, and seemed like the reasonable choice. It was affordable, for one, and while it was in a good location it just seemed like a standard house in a touristy part of the Swiss Alps.

Looking for apartments near Lake Brienz, I came across the Meiringen house. I sent a link to Iain and said it was the exact apartment I'd rent in a perfect world, when I had the money and felt I deserved it. I didn't think that places like this were available to people like me: right by the mountains, built of local wood and with views of waterfalls. How perfect it was made me shy away from getting too excited, and I wasn't sure I could justify the cost.

"If you love it so much, why don't you just ask about it?" asked Iain. "The worst thing you can do is let it go because you haven't asked." With time, I'd come to see just how much his gentle encouragement set my evolution in motion. He showed me that I deserved the courage to ask for what I wanted and dream bigger than I'd allowed myself to until then. That started with seeing if I could make my solitary life in Meiringen a reality.

I sent over an enquiry, and the landlady called me later that day. "How tall are you?" she asked with a New York twang that she explained was from time abroad in her twenties, away from the family home that I wanted to live in more than anything. I told her that the women in my family didn't have a problem with low ceilings, and heard her joy through the phone.

"I've been inundated with enquiries from tall men, when all I've wanted is a nice small woman." We arranged a day for me to see the house, and she offered to take a few hundred francs off the rent.

I knew this was the place for me, and truthfully there was no real reason I shouldn't have it. My job gave me enough for the rent, and if I left or lost that, I'd find a way to get the money from somewhere else. This was one of the first decisions I'd made truly for myself, listening to the murmurs of my own spirit. I felt firmly at the helm of my own life, ready to witness my slow unfolding each day by the mountains.

10

TATZELWURMS

Meiringen is surrounded by lakeside towns. If you hike over the mountains via Brünig-Hasliberg to Lungern, leaving the Berner Oberland for the canton of Obwalden, within a few hours you'll catch sight of the Lungerersee and reach it as you descend to 689m above sea level.

To the west, neighbouring Brienz has the Brienzersee, set in an unthinkably bright blue hue and transparent enough to see the clear cut of the rocks in the shallows as you walk beside it. On my three office days a week, the train I take for my commute to Interlaken runs along its edge. Panoramic windows frame the view for the tourists, cameras snapping as soon as we take the corner onto the water's edge, the lake glittering under the sun on the good days, moody on the stormy ones.

Only the grey-blue Aare river trickles through Meiringen, collecting the glacial meltwater from the waterfalls as it passes and flows towards the Brienzersee. The lack of a larger body of water here could be a flaw, but there's something I like more about being nestled tightly within the valley. It comes with so much more grandeur: the waterfalls for one, the Aare Gorge for another.

It was for the Aare Gorge that I'd been to Meiringen just once before coming here to see the house. You can wander through this 200m-deep geological feat for 1.5km, half expecting dragons to swoop past you breathing fire. It's not a dragon, but a *Tatzelwurm* that found its place in local legend – a snake-like creature with forelegs and teeth. It's now confined to the local bakery, where you can buy an unsettling chocolate-frosted interpretation complete with fangs.

Now I live so close to the gorge, the trees hiding the ravine beneath them visible from my bathroom window and balcony, I visit every few weeks and share the awe of the handful of tourists around me every time. Like everything here that's made of millennia-old rock, it looks different under every light and type of weather. It's never the same.

I first heard about my adopted town long before that, though, in a characteristic way: through books. Meiringen is home to the Reichenbach Falls, the waterfall that Holmes and Moriarty tumble down in "The Final Problem". I can now see it from my dining room window. I smile imagining what my younger Sherlock-reading self would think of where I am now.

So much seems impossible until it happens. But perfect opportunities do exist and when they come into your life, you can either feel unworthy or not ready and push them away, or you can accept them with a heartfelt thank you. It's so easy to say no to everything you've ever wanted. The hardest thing can be to say yes.

TOWARDS THE EASTERN END OF THE AARE GORGE, WHERE
THE ROCKS OPEN UP AND YOU PASS BY WATERFALLS.

THE VIEW OF THE BRIENZERSEE, WALKING TOWARDS
MEIRINGEN FROM THE BRIENZER ROTHORN AT 2,350M. YOU CAN
REACH THE PEAK ON FOOT OR VIA STEAM TRAIN.

11

COFFEE

This is a place made for rituals, the slower and more mindful the better. I love the ritual of coffee as much as the taste. It punctuates my day – once after breakfast, again after lunch.

Choosing the beans and putting them in the grinder. Watching them turn to small fragrant shards. The smell hitting me as I put a scoop into the stove pot.

Finding my favourite cup: small, white and yellow with a chip on the side. Taking it outside to the balcony, where the steam hits the cold morning air. The first sip.

Thank you.

APPROACHING GROSSE SCHEIDEGG, WITH VIEWS OF SOME OF
THE BERNER OBERLAND'S MOST SPECTACULAR MOUNTAINS.

12

VIA ALPINA

My house sits directly on the Red Trail of the Via Alpina, the hiking route all the way across Switzerland that continues through France to Monaco in one direction and Liechtenstein, Austria, Italy and Slovenia to reach Trieste in the other.

The Swiss section is 390km long, from Vaduz in Liechtenstein to Montreux next to the border with France. But that doesn't really tell the full story. The trail takes the scenic route, which in the Alps means there are plenty of mountains along the way: 23,500m of ascents and 24,700m downhill.

If you walk behind my house and through the woods towards Hasliberg, you're heading east, towards Liechtenstein. And if you continue on the path in front of my house, up past the Reichenbach Falls and the mountains I look at every day, you're heading towards Grindelwald and on to Montreux in the west.

The stage from Meiringen to Grindelwald is my challenge for today's hot Saturday weather, and it'll be my first time seeing the Reichenbach Falls up close. Although I've spent a year in Switzerland now, ten months of that in Interlaken and nearly two here, I still haven't done all that much hiking. I felt it was something I needed to be invited to do, rather than just putting my shoes on and heading to the hills. But now, living here alone, there is no one to summon me to put my boots on other than myself.

At 23km, this will be the longest hike I've ever done, but there's something about the Via Alpina that's calling me. Walking over the mountains to Grindelwald – which would otherwise take an hour and a half on the train via Interlaken – is something I know I want to do this year, and the sunny weekends won't go on forever.

I start the route next to my house and continue across the town to the edge of the valley, then through what feels like someone's back garden, vegetable patches with sweet peas and cabbages overflowing their allocated areas. The path enters the edge of the woods on the side of the valley, and continues over rocky, unstable ground under the canopy of trees as the incline begins. Now, deep in summer, the path is overrun with huge ants that are near impossible to avoid standing on, requiring quick hops and course adjustment to reduce the bulk of the damage.

This part of the trail is short but steep and fairly relentless. With today's weather, my pace will absolutely remain a sedate one. The shade of the woodland counts for something, but you only really notice this when you exit it. To reach the waterfall, there are two fields to cross with nowhere to hide from the sun.

At this point, the noise makes it clear the falls are nearby. As I make the final approach and get my first glimpse of the water, I'm left with the strange feeling of being intimate with something I know so well from afar. I felt like I knew the waterfall just from looking out of my dining room window. But up close, I realise I don't know it well at all.

Here, it's crashing and aggressive, with no tempering from the gentler surrounding landscape. The mist comes in waves. It's refreshing when you first arrive, worn out from the hike, but outside the peak of summer I know it will be enough to make you eager to move on.

From my house, there's no way of seeing the Sherlock Society's plaque with a brief explanation of its history, nor the "danger of death" sign to keep eager tourists away from the edge. From afar, you can't sense how much power there is in the water. Meiringen relies on hydropower, and here you can absolutely see how. It's ruthless.

I sit on the steep bank with a few dandelions and buttercups dotted across the grass, and marvel at the noise as the falls crash against the rocks below. The water foams where it hits the rock and creates the cloud of thin mist that travels back up to hit my face. I stay still and watch, feeling the mist on my skin as the wind blows. I breathe in, trying to make the moment last.

From here, it's a few hours to Grosse Scheidegg, the highest point of this stage of the Via Alpina. Then it's over the other side and down to Grindelwald. Just a few kilometres up the trail, I sit huffing and puffing on a boulder at the side of the path, tomato-red and wondering how on earth I can manage what I've calculated to be a minimum of seven more hours of walking.

One thing I'll learn in the next three years is that I always find a way. No matter how hard it gets, there's some sort of magic involved in putting one foot in front of another up a mountain. I always get there – and I will today. Despite the red-faced breathlessness and my heartbeat echoing through every limb, I know this is just the start of my relationship with the mountains.

After I get back to my house that evening, shovel down food and shower, I dig out a small A4 map of Switzerland that came with my rail pass to show the train routes. In black marker, I draw a small line from Meiringen to Grindelwald, no more than a centimetre on the map, and pin it to the wooden panelling outside my bathroom door. The space either side of the line to the eastern and western borders of Switzerland looks back at me. I have work to do.

" The torrent, swollen by the melting snow, plunges into a tremendous abyss, from which the spray rolls up like the smoke from a burning house. The shaft into which the river hurls itself is an immense chasm, lined by glistening, coal-black rock, and narrowing into a creaming, boiling pit of incalculable depth, which brims over and shoots the stream onward over its jagged lip. The long sweep of green water roaring for ever down, and the thick flickering curtain of spray hissing for ever upwards, turn a man giddy with their constant whirl and clamour. "

SIR ARTHUR CONAN DOYLE,
DESCRIBING THE REICHENBACH FALLS
IN THE FINAL PROBLEM

13
LIFE

This place is working its magic on me. My morning routine is to sit on my balcony and let the sound of the waterfalls and the birds soothe me. It's more comfortable to sit out here than on the springy sofa in the dining room, and the view is better anyway. I put my legs up on the wooden frame in front of me, look around and fill my lungs with morning air.

Stillness can feel so alien when you have drifted on a current of unease for so long. Catching a glimpse of peace and letting it stay a while feels like new and uncomfortable territory at first, until you realise the quiet is what the safety of the shore looks like.

I spent so many years in a state of fight or flight, running from an imaginary bear that started chasing me when I was fourteen. Back then, I felt so flawed. I was convinced I would never be enough – pretty enough, clever enough, funny enough – and I didn't respond with kindness. I took my pain out on myself and did everything I could to hide who I really was. I wanted to be invisible, to fade away into nothingness without anyone noticing I had gone.

It became serious when I was fifteen, and just making a phone call or going to the shops made me more anxious than I could ever describe to others. I dreaded having attention on me in class and feeling like I was being judged; that everyone's eyes were on my flaws. I just wanted it to end. If only I could have found the exits I know now: into nature and the beauty around me, with a gentle patience and knowledge that it will someday pass.

Back then, I was instead living a strange dichotomy: while consistently at the top of my classes and applying for Oxford University, I was also destroying myself by barely eating and dating people eight years older than me. One evening, I sat on my bed, pulled a razor blade apart and carved a heart shape into the side of my left wrist, blood outlining the shape for a moment before pooling into a small amorphous red sea. Years on, after so much has changed, I can still see the right curved line when I'm cold. No one else can, but I know exactly where to look for it.

I've thought back to why I did that and the many other analogues of hurting myself. I don't think I wanted others to know I needed help. In hindsight, I think I just wanted to suffer. I wanted to morph the pain I was feeling inside into something real and legitimately painful. Pain that had a logical reason for it and could be fixed with antiseptic and a plaster.

I wish I could tell myself that it was temporary, like all of the other forms of suffering I'd feel from that moment on; some misty clouds of nothingness, others angry lightning storms and deep seas pulling me down from all sides. I wish I knew then that I was allowed to feel pain and that I would find help. That my way out of the darkness would always be giving myself love and care and gentleness before anyone else would. By taking it one day at a time, noticing the sun and the breeze and the neighbour's happy dog on his walk and the taste of marmite on toast. Getting through one day and another, slowly noticing that it's a fraction better than before.

At the start of my degree at Exeter University, I started getting help because I could: I wasn't dependent on my parents to understand that there was a problem and take me to a therapist. But healing would be a long journey.

In one Spanish language seminar, I was called on to read out a section from a book and couldn't get my words out. I sat there frozen as the class waited in silence. I tried to speak and my breath caught in my throat. My heart rate careened upwards and I tried to breathe again, and again. Tears falling, I got up and ran out the room. I sat down in the empty print room and put my head in my hands as my body heaved through it. A girl from the seminar came in with my bag and books, sat down next to me and put her arm around me. "It's okay," she said. "Just let it out. It's okay."

Everyone else seemed so normal and well-functioning; I was sure that they'd never have to go through this. I told my university supervisor that I couldn't go back to my seminars and he explained that it could mean I wouldn't graduate. At that moment, I didn't care. Someone in the administration took pity on me and I finished the next summer with a first-class degree and commendation. Looking at my graduation certificate and photos feels laughable to me: on the surface, you really do have no idea what's going on in someone's life.

Now at twenty-three, only a handful of years after I wasn't sure I could ever get through university, let alone forge the life I wanted, I'm here in the mountains. Gradually, I notice that I'm letting my body open up to slower and more rejuvenating rhythms of life. I've only been here a few months, but I've already spent so much time just sitting and watching the world. By slowing down and letting go, things are changing deep inside. Clouds are parting and the weather is settling.

Bravery can show up in a multitude of ways. It's not all fighting danger and bellowing for freedom. The smallest and quietest choices can be the boldest moments – to no longer tolerate what's holding us down, to commit to shining brighter and to jump wholeheartedly into the rip current of living.

But there are still echoes of my past. Sometimes I feel like I'm painting over the hairline cracks of my low confidence and self-doubt rather than looking at them head on, feeling their full extent deep under the surface and solving them. My weak points are clearest in my relationship. Every few months, the same thing happens: Iain says or does something harmless that tugs at my doubt, and I spiral.

He talks about a girl he works with who's clever and funny and kind, and I am certain she would make him happier than I ever could. The easiest answer, I tell myself, is that I will never be good enough. And it'd be better for everyone if I was alone, so I could only fuck up my own life. I pull away from him, look the other way, go silent and don't let him touch me. I drift away into a cold, numb and disconnected place far away from him. And I feel strangely safe there.

This isn't one of those days, however. It's been a happy weekend with Iain: two days of hiking and lazy breakfasts and wine on the balcony at night. Iain left a few hours ago and the house is now back to its usual quiet with just one proprietor keeping watch. I walk inside and look at the mountains from my dining room as the day is ending with a bang, the pink tones of alpenglow reflected on the mountain as the sun sets. I think about how far I've come already, where I'm heading and how I'll spend my time in this house. Without sheer terror of the world in my way, what shall I do with my life?

Here in the silence and surrounded by mountains, I'm starting to find my answers, at least for now. I want to be moulded by the world: by the people I've loved and the places I've sat and listened quietly, watching leaves falling, the sun rising and stars appearing. I hope to make it all worth it. I want to write about the beauty I notice on my journey, read widely and open my eyes as I step outside my corner of the world. And with time, if I'm lucky, I invite the mountains, galaxies and sand dunes to show in the furrows on my face.

THE VIEW FROM MY BALCONY OF THE
BÄNZLAUISTOCK AND RESTITURM
CASTLE RUINS.

" Walk away quietly in any direction and taste the freedom of the mountaineer. Camp out among the grasses and gentians of glacial meadows, in craggy garden nooks full of nature's darlings. "

JOHN MUIR

14

AFTERNOON WALKS

Since I started my job in Interlaken, the company has quickly grown – and so has my role. I'm managing a group of ten people writing, translating and designing. I love the process of creation: having an outcome that needs to be achieved and setting all the pieces in motion to make it happen. Most of the people in my team are older than me, and I try not to make an issue out of it. I want to collaborate on one level, not demand order. "You need to be aggressive," another manager tells me one morning by the coffee machine, "otherwise you'll never be respected."

I'm becoming more conscious of the blurred boundary between my own real yearnings and those I've adopted from the one-size-fits-all checklist. A good job. Managing people. Leading a company. A big salary and house. The boxes to tick and impress people with, doing exactly what I'm meant to be doing at the right time. I like the satisfaction I get when I improve the numbers and bring in results. But it's an empty success. I leave my house just before eight in the morning, get back for eight in the evening, make dinner, shower and go to sleep not long after. There's little space for projects and imagination and dreaming outside of work, and I do not have the energy for it anyway. I push myself to write on weekends, but it's like my brain is stuck in treacle, wanting to just sit and enjoy the view instead.

I only have so much energy in my tank, and so much of it is going to a place that isn't important to me. When did I ever decide I wanted this?

All I ever really wanted was to dream, make things and explore. Now I realise just how desperate I am to get back to those basic things that are worth so much more than my salary. I want to spend afternoons surrounded by the forest and look forward to nights under the stars. To wander off the footpath to enjoy the view and identify the birds of prey over the valley. To ignore the timelines and priorities I don't care about and live on my own terms. How possible that is, I'm not sure. But it feels like there could be no better foundation for the rest of my life than existing quietly, right now, with the wilderness at my feet.

On weekends and the days I work from home, I've got into the habit of heading to the woods on the mountainside above my house in the afternoon. I stop often, crouching down to feel the soft ground underfoot and touch the rocks and mosses, which are always cooler than everything else around them.

For much of my life, the woods have been my escape. Next to the house my parents built together – a converted oast house, once used for drying hops and with a mysterious tower of circular rooms topped by a white-tipped cowl – was ten acres of unkempt woodland on the border of our sixty acres of farmland. I'd retreat there alone at nine years old, worrying my mother senseless. But I hadn't felt an explanation was needed: I was adventuring, exploring and searching for discoveries... new paths, dens in hedgerows, a deer foal, or a tree struck by lightning.

Although our houses changed after my parents divorced when I was nine, the proximity and therapy of trees remained. At my dad's next two homes, as I was unravelling in my new reality of parents who couldn't and wouldn't love each other, I'd wake up long before everyone else to run down the road and into the woods. I can't remember why I started doing this; I felt drawn to it somehow. And soon I knew I needed it.

I have started doing the same here. Some days it's a slow walk, stopping often to look at what's underfoot or in the forest canopy above, but on others I sprint downhill through the trees that run along the edge of the mountain and bounce off the rocks, finding that speed is a far better insulator against bumpy terrain than caution. Exercise has nothing to do with these moments. It's always been about the wind in my face, the companionship of the whispering trees in their own close-knit society and the sound of my heart in my body. Freedom.

I stop to put my hand on the huge boulder that marks the beginning and end of my circuit through the woods, guarding the trail like a Japanese *torii* gate at the transition from the mundane to the divine. Ferns grow in a jagged crack through its middle, relishing the cool dampness and stretching towards a glimmer of sun.

WALKING THROUGH THE WOODS BEHIND
MY HOUSE, NEAR THE RESTITURM RUINS.

15
SEASONS

As summer eases into autumn, the shape of my days changes. On warm days, I have been going on long hikes in the mountains to watch the valleys burning orange and auburn below. On cooler days, I just pack a few more layers. But life is becoming cosier and more introspective.

There's something about the changing of the season that calls out for time to pause and reassess. I make tea more often, especially the local Alpine blends from the supermarket with lemon balm, orange mint, goldenrod and nettle. It reminds me of the warm, sweet and woody smell of the house that I notice most when I've been away for a few days.

I spend afternoons doing nothing but reading, or bring my fleecy blanket out onto the balcony to sit and write in my journal. Finding inspiration further east, I remember how much I love baking with cinnamon and cardamom. Around me, nature is retreating too. As the leaves fall, there's busyness in the air as squirrels pad out their stores and birds reinforce their nests. Everyone's direction is inwards: into our homes and towards warmth, comfort and rest.

AUTUMN DAYS SPENT TRYING TO MASTER THE ART OF SCANDINAVIAN BAKING.

16

TRAUMHAUS

Iain has started calling the house my *Traumhaus*, or dream house, and the name has stuck. He loves being here as much as I do, and we talk about how we'd like to live together someplace like this in future. Not right now, with Iain working in his lab in Zurich for the next few years until he gets his PhD, but someday.

It's here that I've come to find a warm and comfortable home for myself, both physically and mentally. I feel peaceful, and I'm not sure when I last felt this – or if I really ever have in adulthood. During the mornings, the light streams through my balcony door and makes its way into the kitchen. I grind coffee beans, heat water, find my blanket and enjoy the sun on my face before finding a book to curl up with for an hour or so, the steam from the coffee dancing in the cold morning air.

Early on Sundays, I sit here to listen to the long, wavering sound of alphorns gliding across the valley. A couple that look in their sixties meet up on the hill most weekends, somewhere in the forest. They always play the same melody, one that's traditional here in the Berner Oberland and so slow and mournful. When the valley is encased in mist, the notes perfectly match the movements of the clouds over the mountains and the breeze through the forest as blackbirds dance between the trees. Up until their last note, everything in their universe and mine as listener is in perfect alignment.

From my cushions, I look over to the exposed rock face of the Bänzlauistock and the contours of the still snowy Gelmerhörner far beyond on the horizon, 15km southeast from here. Closer by, trees line the Aare Gorge, and higher up, elevated above the valley on green rural banks, is the little hamlet of Geissholz, marked by a pylon that flashes red to warn off low-flying military jets. And further behind is Innertkirchen.

Innertkirchen is even less of an urban centre than Meiringen, but I love walking over the mountain to get there. It's just a few kilometres from here on a map but with the mountains standing firmly in the way, it feels like a completely different place. In the centre of the village, there's one thing I look forward to that nonetheless always takes me by surprise: a vast and imposing rock face on one side of the valley, with a fierce drop that fills me in equal measures with dread and wonder. While the valley edges in Meiringen are straight out of a landscape painting, all waterfalls and glacier-tipped mountains, this cliff face is the stuff of fantasy novels. Whether friend or foe, you would be faced with a terrifying drop if you dared to climb it.

A train now burrows through the mountains, breaking down the barriers between the two villages with a seven-minute journey that feels almost laughable in comparison with the hike. But that would be missing out on the sunlight greeting you through the trees, the waterfall in the clearing that's perfect for a quick dip in summer, and the neatly stacked logs in the forest before the path starts dropping down into the Innertkirchen valley. So much more is gained by taking the longer scenic route.

ON MY WAY OVER THE MOUNTAINS TO
INNERTKIRCHEN FROM MEIRINGEN.

17
SHOWERS

I love the bathroom here: it's small but always warm, and the view reaches over my balcony towards the former Gadmen municipality, now part of Innertkirchen, and the jagged lines of the Gelmerhörner.

I've found that showers are best spent when you're soapy, just under the cusp of being too hot, and can see the contours of a mountain through the steam. Out of the window, the first snow of the year is settling.

I step out the shower and look at the mirror front of the bathroom cabinet, where I've started leaving Post-it notes with quotes I've stumbled upon in books and wanted to remember. Right now, the final lines from Mary Oliver's "The Summer Day" are looking back at me. Early on this winter Saturday morning, I wonder what it is I'll do with my one wild and precious life.

18

JOY

I read Wordsworth and think about what makes my heart leap up.

The first light of morning pouring through the balcony door and into the kitchen. Freshly ground coffee. An open bottle of red wine on the table. Hot midday showers. Getting into bed early to read. Sitting outside and watching the moon under a blanket. Wanting to drop everything to continue reading a good book – and then finding the perfect moment to do just that.

MY BALCONY IN WINTER, LOOKING IN THE DIRECTION OF THE AARE GORGE AND, FURTHER BEYOND, INNERTKIRCHEN AND THE GELMERHÖRNER.

19
WHY, WHY, WHY

I read *A Little Life* by Hanya Yanagihara and it destroys me.

20

THE ORANGERIE

Just next to my kitchen is the dining room – it's decently sized, but a room that I pass through more than anything else. I sometimes read on the sofa or work at the dining table, but not habitually. Iain and I sometimes jokingly call it the Orangerie or the Sunday room; there's something of a regal air to it, especially when the light beams through the windows in the late hours of the afternoon.

However, the view from these windows is perhaps the best in the house. You could argue for all of my views, but this one has the Reichenbach Falls in its favour. Above the Reichenbach Falls there's the Wetterhorn, which a nineteen-year-old Winston Churchill climbed in 1894, the Wellhorn and the Rosenlaui glacier in between. To the left of these, you can see the finger-like contours of the 4km-long Engelhörner range, translating literally as "Angel Horns".

Gertrude Bell, the British adventurer, spy, ancient historian, Middle Eastern linguist and a thousand other things, travelled to the Berner Oberland in 1901, first climbing the 4,078m Schreckhorn. She then set herself a challenge to climb all of the perpendicular peaks of the Engelhörner range, the same mountains I see from my bedroom window every morning as soon as I wake up. Over two weeks, she scaled each one, one after another, and claimed seven virgin peaks. One of these was named after her – Gertrudespitze (Gertrude's Peak).

When I look at these mountains, I often think of her. Courage lives on in the contours of the earth. I look at the rocks still standing, long after Gertrude Bell died in 1926, and think of her arduous days on the rope, her exhausted glory while looking at the Haslital below, and her life to come. At just fifty-seven, Gertrude Bell would overdose on sleeping pills in her bedroom in Baghdad. Sick and frail and with a possible case of lung cancer, Gertrude had once been one of the finest mountaineers of her time, but that was just a tiny fraction of her life.

She travelled through Greater Syria, Mesopotamia, Asia Minor and Arabia and forged bonds that would help establish and administer the modern state of Iraq. After long days in the saddle, she translated poems by Rumi and negotiated with desert tribes. During World War I, she was asked by British Intelligence to help soldiers through the deserts. All before women got the vote back home in the United Kingdom.

I wonder how we can achieve everything we want while still fulfilling our real needs; of staying happy, healthy and loved. Of balancing ambition and the other truly important building blocks of a life. I look up to the mountains and feel supported by them somehow, like we're in this together. I love knowing their past and their good and bad sides; having the intimacy of seeing them in every type of weather and all times of day. I see them, and they see me.

THE MOUNTAIN VIEW FROM MY DINING ROOM
UNDER A CLOUD OF EVENING ALPENGLOW.

ALPEN-ENZIAN, OR GENTIAN

watching
the world

66 ...a rosy glow, at first scarce discernible, gradually

deepened and suffused every mountain-top,

flushing the glaciers and the harsh crags above

them. This was the alpenglow, to me the most

impressive of all the terrestrial manifestations

of God. At the touch of this divine light, the

mountains seemed to kindle to a rapt, religious

consciousness, and stood hushed like devout

worshippers waiting to be blessed. 99

JOHN MUIR

21

WINTER

The trees outside my kitchen window stand at the foot of the Hasliberg ski resort and every half hour in peak season you can see a cable car pass over the branches. Down the mountainside runs a waterfall, but only after heavy rain and with the melting snow in spring. There is a small stream running year-round, though, letting the sound of water flow into the kitchen when the windows are open. At the point where the waterfall joins the stream, it's louder and stronger, sweeping away whatever's in its path and carrying it into the Aare.

Living next to a ski lift, you'd think that I'd go up the mountain all the time. The truth is a bit different. But once a week or so in winter, I love going up there on the first cable car of the day, with fresh snow and no one else around. After the awkward shuffle in ski boots over the bridge and to the lift, first up is the cable car to Reuti. Then, it's out of the cable car and into a gondola to head up to Mägisalp, where kids grab their sledges and follow the trail to look for dwarves in the forest. If you want to go further up to Hasliberg, you can choose whether to take another gondola or the chairlift from here.

Navigating the universes of ski lifts and walking in uncomfortable boots isn't new to me, although I was out of practice when I moved here. After my mum left my dad when I was nine or ten, she went off to the Pyrenees to become a ski instructor. With our lives split halfway between each of theirs, this meant winters in the mountains and learning to ski. My younger brother and sister and I joined two boys, the kids of the ski school bosses, to form our mountain crew, and headed off every morning to terrorise the pistes, resurfacing sometime around lunch at the ski school restaurant.

I was the eldest, just turned sixteen at the end of the winters we spent there, and didn't have quite the same fearlessness as my nine-year-old brother. Together with the boys, he'd push off, tuck himself in as small as his already tiny body could be, and straight-line the resort's new black run before breaking into a screeching halt approaching the tree line at the end of the piste. My pace then was much more sedate, as it is now. My family always joked that I ski like I'm doing my supermarket shopping, which I've never questioned too much. Sedate is fine for me.

AT THE TOP OF HASLIBERG.

WATCHING THE SUN RISE ABOVE THE
MOUNTAINS ON A MORNING SKI.

From Monday to Wednesday I commute along the lake to my office in Interlaken, while on Thursdays and Fridays I set up my office at my kitchen counter, close to the kettle and whatever I've baked recently. As long as I'm at my laptop to start work at nine o'clock, anything goes.

On some mornings, I get the early cable car to the top and take the slow route down. I make deep turns and curve into the snow while sweeping around the wide corners, turning just before the tree line where the piste machine has left powder. I relax my knees and let my legs bounce off the contours of the mountain, the snow throwing me wherever it wants to. I love getting that feeling back every winter.

All that said, on more days than not, I try to block out the sound of awkward footsteps in ski boots clattering around outside my bedroom window. I pull my duvet up and admire the view of the snow-capped Engelhörner from my cosy vantage point. That's another good way to enjoy a mountain town in winter.

22

CUISINE

This evening I fry thinly-sliced and salted potatoes to make *rösti*. I serve a fried runny egg on top and, reaping the rewards of a rare well-stocked fridge, sprinkle over chopped chives with coarse black pepper and salt.

Before visiting Switzerland the first time in 2015 to see Iain, I had never had Swiss food. That was one of the worlds he introduced me to: one abundant in cheese, potatoes and pickles.

I've never bought a fondue pot for my house, and I think it'll stay that way. Despite a wonderful range of bad habits, I value my arteries too much for more than a few mouthfuls once a year. But sometimes when Iain visits me here, or on the rare evenings when friends from work are invited, I get out the two raclette grills I picked up at the supermarket not long after moving here.

Usually two people share each grill, choosing their own selection of mushrooms, onions, peppers, pears and pickles, plus strips of meat for the carnivores. Underneath the top grill, there's space to put our personal cheese trays, which after a few minutes will melt and start bubbling.

Each armed with our own little grill tool, we turn our vegetables and check the consistency of our cheese. When everything starts coming together, I drizzle the cheese from my tray atop hot boiled potatoes on my plate and add the grilled accompaniments that are ready, turning the rest so they're ready for the next round.

It happens rarely, but I like this type of evening. As everyone creates their ideal combination of food and competes for the best grill status and cheese consistency, the focus is taken off me as the host and I can slip more easily into the background.

23
RESTITURM

My balcony looks out onto the ruins of a thirteenth-century castle, the Restiturm; once home to the Hasli knights, vassals of the Habsburgs.

Overlooking the whole of the Haslital valley, it served to control and protect the valley and the trade routes across the Grimselpass, Jochpass, Sustenpass, Grosse Scheidegg and Brünigpass. Now, these are my well-trodden hiking paths. The renovation signs explain that the castle was constructed inside out, with the core's construction beginning in 1250. The tower I'm looking at now took another fifty years to complete.

At night, the tower is illuminated so you can see every contour, including the turrets and slit windows for fending off attackers. Sitting here on my balcony, an archer would be able to defeat me in a second.

Orion rises above the Restiturm before moving west, towards my bedroom window. Before I go to sleep I have a habit of looking out of my windows one at a time. I start with the balcony, checking how the castle looks; sometimes deep under mist, other nights under an intricate starry quilt. I breathe in and out, using this ritual as my reminder to slow down and stop holding so much tension that doesn't serve me. I walk through the kitchen to the dining room to see if I can spot the moon and head to my bedroom, switching off the lights on my way so darkness eventually fills the house.

I look for Orion's belt of three bright stars and his sword below. I remember that the sword is the key to orienting yourself; of using the night sky as your natural navigator. The sword is pointing directly downwards. I'm looking south.

To the right of Orion lie Taurus and the Pleiades, sometimes called the Seven Sisters. That cluster of stars that has always seemed so bright to me, even before I knew what it was called. I always look for it. I feel joy when I find it.

Sometimes after nightfall, I walk down the road to the farmland near the Aare Gorge where the streetlights are sparse and the sky is clearest. I'm always undisturbed as I stand or sit there. Looking up at the quiet stars in the blackness, the only sound is the rustle of the sheep stirring against the hay in their sheds. Set against that unfathomable canvas, earthly problems are shrunk down to the size they should be.

I get in bed and leave my curtain half open, as I always do. From my pillow I can see a few bright stars to the south-east. I feel my body sink down into the bed and I pay attention to my place in the world. I feel the

ground below me and the stars above me. I think about the air pumping
through my lungs. Tomorrow the sun will come up and shine
on me. I'll live and breathe as just one more part of this world.

THE VIEW FROM MY BALCONY BEFORE
NIGHTFALL IN WINTER, THE MOON
JUST ABOVE THE BÄNZLAUISTOCK.

24
HUMAN GUESTS

I see Iain most weekends now, taking turns between me going to the city and him coming to the mountains. We like that balance. I go to Zurich for city life and coffee shops and restaurants for Middle Eastern food and Thai curry, and he comes here to retreat into his therapy house by the Alps. When he's here, we have equal parts laziness and enjoying the outdoors, heading out on a day hike after a late breakfast, then returning to sit on the balcony with a beer before making dinner together.

A few other friends have joined me here, but only a handful of people a handful of times. Truthfully, I thrive like this: a distance away from the life of the party, hidden next to the woods in a little house overlooking the mountains. People idealise this kind of life, but in reality, I don't think it's what most people want.

The few people I am close to here are special to me, though – and admirably persistent too. Most of my friendships are built on the foundations of the other person repeatedly ignoring my wish for privacy and forcing me to spend time with them until I eventually relent, realising that I do in fact like them a lot.

Ruben shares my love for the mountains, adventure and wild journeys, and wanders off to places like Kyrgyzstan while I explore the Arctic. Sometimes we go to the climbing gym and he gives me a small preview of what he does on his own, climbing big mountains, including the big three across the valley: the Eiger, Mönch and Jungfrau. I wonder if I'll ever have a chance to learn this too. For now, I can just about make it to the top of the climbing wall, powered by Snickers bars. Other times we just go to the Mexican restaurant and order margaritas while comparing notes on life.

MY HOUSE IN WINTER, SEEN FROM
THE BRIDGE ACROSS THE STREAM.

But most of the time, I'm alone. I turn down most social invites. I take awkwardness to impressive heights. I'm living a weird life and doing what I'm not meant to be doing in my twenties. But increasingly, anything else would feel like such a profound disappointment to my own expectations of myself.

Even as I become more carefree and ignore more of the social codes that I once tried so hard to follow, I still feel gaps in my confidence. I grew up shy, and the years of anxiety and self-doubt are not far behind me and yet to fully heal. Even here, there are echoes of the old fear that once filled all of the spaces in my days. I still blush in meetings when I'm asked a question and feel my palms sweating when it's nearly my turn to speak. And when my skin is bad with the acne I've never managed to fully solve, I try even harder to hide my face and stay invisible.

I wonder if this house will help me find more balance and reassurance that I'm worthy of my own love and others', or if my solitude risks a spiral back to where I was. For now, I breathe in and look out the window as nature carries on. Today, I'm happy.

THE MOUNTAINS IN THE CLOUDS
AFTER SNOW IN DECEMBER.

25
MARCH

It's early morning and it's snowing. The blackbirds are flitting between the trees. Not much snow has settled yet. The roads are clear, but there's a dusty build-up on the tree branches, not quite enough to cause a bend in their structures. I wonder what it will look like this evening and where the blackbirds will be keeping warm.

I've spent a lot of time sitting at this kitchen counter, looking out of the window or at words on pages. I've thought how this would be the perfect place to write a book. It's got all the right characteristics of a place a writer would want to barricade themselves in, with ample doses of pleasure and focus. A season here with days spent writing on the balcony, watching the mountains and dreaming about their histories and futures, and afternoons spent roaming the woods.

It's also deathly quiet. I love this, but it's not for everyone. My sister spent the night here on her own and blocked the bedroom door shut with her suitcase. She hated the quiet and didn't want to look at the empty darkness beyond the bedroom at night.

I'd love to give my house keys to an artist, to tell them to put their phone in a box, turn off the internet I got installed when I moved here and get inspired by the views and create. Perhaps I should be passing on the message to myself; to sit here with my pen and paper more often and just see what pours out.

APPROACHING THE CHURCH ON MY WALK
INTO MEIRINGEN ON A SNOWY DAY.

26

TO THE MOUNTAINS

I wish I could stand as firm as you

Not moving one bit when the wind howls

Taking it as it comes

Standing tall, confident and strong

Battered from the years and the bad weather.

Today I will try.

A WEEKEND GLACIER TREK FROM AROLLA TO
THE GLACIER DE CHEILON, OVERNIGHTING AT
THE CABANE DES DIX.

KAMIKOCHI IN THE JAPANESE ALPS.

27
HEAT

I love being warm and turning up the temperature dial of the shower as hot as I can manage. But not for too long. I'm too pale and redheaded to stand it for more than a few minutes. I love the idea of sitting in a sauna, but the reality is I just can't hack it.

On a trip to Japan with Iain, I knew I wanted to try a traditional *onsen*, or natural hot spring bath. We chose one in Kamikochi, one of the most beautiful parts of the country in the middle of the Japanese Alps. It's funny that: after holidaying to the other side of the world, I still gravitate to the Alps. The mountains here feel like cousins of my Swiss ones back home, carved by glaciers over millennia, although the difference is marked by their lack of Alpen meadows and rustic farmland on their edges. The sound of cowbells won't ring out here.

The rivers remind me most of Switzerland: glacial blue-grey, completely clear and painfully cold. The *onsen* is just by the lake in the heart of Kamikochi. From where you bathe, you can only see the trees above; but still, you know you are in an incredible part of the world.

I got to the *onsen* changing room and undressed, sat on one of the stools to shower and scrub, and walked outside to the pools. I sat naked with a few Japanese women, water of up to forty degrees Celsius reaching our shoulders. Some of the pools were like whisky barrels, with a small ladder to get in and only room for one person at a time.

This is like what a Haruki Murakami character would do, I thought. And I loved it too. Being outside with nothing on, in beautifully hot water, looking up at the forest in mountain territory. But after fifteen minutes, my face – and most of my body, I expect – was tomato-red. The colour of my skin wouldn't go down for the rest of the afternoon.

28
COLD

The first time I swam in freezing cold water was in the Arctic in 2017, all in the name of getting a certificate for the Arctic Naked Bathing Club from Longyearbyen Campsite in Svalbard. Like the *onsen* in Kamikochi, I was in my birthday suit, but this time the water running through Longyearbyen was nearly forty degrees Celsius cooler. After about thirty seconds, my body felt like it was turning numb and my joints stopped behaving as I knew they should. I paddled around for as long as I needed to get the certificate, and tripped trying to step over the slippery rocks to get out. My skin was pink and felt like tiny needles were pricking me all over. But I got to appreciate the main difference between hot and freezing water: that the cold makes you feel so incredibly alive.

When I got back to Switzerland, we went swimming in the river that runs right next to my office, the Aare. Like the river in Kamikochi, the Aare is cooled by the glacial meltwater that trickles off the mountains above it, so even in summer it's still cold. Afterwards, I asked my friend Ruben if he'd be up for swimming in the river throughout the winter with me, perhaps once a month. "Yes, but once a week," he said. We made a date, every Wednesday at 9.30 a.m., and set up a scoring system and record sheet for others in the office to join in. We'd sneak out the office to swim twenty-two weeks that winter, turning up to the water's edge every week with whoever we could convince to join us and swimsuits under our clothes.

In January, I wear my down jacket, snow boots and thick winter layers. Next to the river, I take everything off and I am standing there in just my swimsuit, my paper-white skin goose-pimpled all over. I step onto the rock where we always start, try to ease into the water as fast as I can and feel the shock of the cold all over. After the first few strokes it gets easier, but soon after that your body gets increasingly numb. When I reach the rock that marks the finish, I pull myself out of the water and walk back to our clothes and the towel that I've laid out, so cold my skin is burning hot. "You're mad," passers-by on their morning walk next to the river tell us week after week, "absolutely insane."

We often debate whether it's best to ease in gradually, as I like to, or dive straight in and surface from the water with your body in shock, your body gasping for air. I will never jump in – I can't bear it. I'd rather go in slowly and feel every ounce of pain as the water edges up my body. Any day.

THE SITE OF OUR AARE SWIMMING CLUB, WHERE I SWAM
EVERY WEEK FROM OCTOBER 2017 TO APRIL 2018.

29
STRENGTH

Even now, I care too much about the reflection that looks back at me. I look sadly at the bumpy skin on my legs and the lines on my thighs that are even whiter than the skin around them. I see it as a moral failing when my skin isn't flawless. I forget how strong I am, how I can climb mountains, hang from things and pull up the weight of my body, and submerge myself in the lake at the coldest time of year.

I judge myself on what isn't right according to photographs of beautiful women I'm led to believe are normal and let my sense of self become fainter and smaller. I forget how I love people without really giving thought to their appearance at all, how I adore and appreciate their quirks as a beautiful part of them without even seeing them as flaws. I forget to be my own friend and treat myself as my loved ones do.

Eastern philosophies talk about mind-body connections. I ponder my body and self-worth connection, how I think, "Because I am beautiful, I am deserving. Because I am flawed, I have a poor moral character." I would say that for a smart person I can be pretty fucking stupid, but that would not be being kind to myself.

BEGINNING THE DAY HIKING FROM THE BLÜEMLISALPHÜTTE, THE
MOUNTAIN HUT ABOVE KANDERSTEG AND THE OESCHINENSEE.
PHOTO BY STEFAN TSCHUMI FOR SWITZERLAND TOURISM.

A GREAT TIT, WITH THE WHITE BACKDROP OF THE
ENGELHÖRNER BEHIND THE TREES.

30

It's one of the first warm days of spring. It feels too warm, like summer. Everyone I pass looks like they're remembering what summer felt like, and as if they're wondering whether they should trust it – coats still flung over their arm. On my way back from the supermarket I stop opposite Meiringen church, where there's a little fountain and space to sit. The three long benches, each constructed of half a tree trunk and positioned in a circle, give it an ancient feeling, like pagan worship could take place here under the overhanging tree.

At quarter past three, the church bell sounds and two old ladies, one a bit less old and guiding the other, sit down on an adjacent bench. I get up after a minute or so, trying to smile and look like they hadn't made me leave. For now I want solitude.

I get home and sit on my balcony, on my own again and watching the birds. A golden eagle is swooping the sky, taking ownership of all the blue space I can see from here. Birds of prey belong here in the mountains. I love watching them dive with a controlled, graceful strength, especially when they are in pairs, encircling each other's paths in a private dance far, far above me.

On the largest tree I can see from here, with just the early buds of spring showing, there were two citril finches this morning. Now there's a single great tit, graceful and neat in his delicate colours. I go to get my camera and he's gone when I'm back. I wait a bit longer. He returns, singing to spring, and I get a photo. The backdrop of the Engelhörner range is behind him, out of focus and blurred white.

I think that a place with birds singing is something like paradise. I look at the birds and think of their freedom, how they can fly anywhere they choose. And then there are their colours, their song. What better role models to inspire a life?

31

WHEN I AM FEELING LOW

Please remind me of all the times I've been

high on the magic of this world.

It's still here.

Look up as night falls,

Wait for the stars.

32
SAYING GOODNIGHT

I get home from a meal with Stephen in Interlaken after work, slightly drunk, and look up at the stars from my bedroom window, as I do most days before bed. I fall in love with the night sky again and again, especially here where there's so little light pollution. Tonight there's a dark, spangly quilt without a single cloud, the moon a slim yellow cut-out throwing just a slither of light through my curtains.

Unusually for nearly midnight, I don't feel tired, and head out to my balcony with a blanket. For about half an hour, I lie here and watch the brightest stars above the Restiturm castle ruins on the hill. On the Grimsel mountain range in the distance, I can see the remnants of the winter's snow glimmering under the night sky.

I think for a while about life, the people I've met through my job, and how I'll miss it here when it comes to leaving. I think about how the stars are one of my favourite things, even ahead of the mountains sometimes. Then I say goodnight to the constellations and head to bed.

33
WORK

For the last few weeks, I've been watching a great tit I first spotted here earlier this month. He's taken up residence on the trunk of the large tree next to my balcony. He sings his two-syllable song and sometimes his partner responds, her song muffled in the distance. They keep swooping back to their nest, where I imagine little mouths stretched wide open.

Alongside my nine-to-seven job over in Interlaken, sitting in an office at a desk, albeit one with a view of the mountains, sometimes I feel like my real job is to stay in touch with the nature here around my home. I think I'm doing quite well. I know the birds, their calls and where they nest. As the day changes, I track the sun across the sky and watch the moon rise. I get to know the constellations.

While living here, my commitment is to stillness and quiet noticing: of the bee rumbling with focus to finish its job in the neighbour's rose garden and the unravelling bud on the scarlet geranium on an otherwise uneventful afternoon.

I'm reminded of the value of the most basic things: tending to our body, home, and the humans and good creatures we enjoy our lives with. To live and love and be present for it all. Cool forest air, mountainsides alight with alpenglow and the first evening stars coming into focus. It can hardly be called living simply when it's worth so much.

When something changes, I notice it. I watch the tree buds stretch out into green leaves, the reddish swell of cones on the Swiss pine and an extra-yellow moon rise over the valley. I feel in touch with the natural world and it heals me.

A BEE ON THE MEADOWS ABOVE MEIRINGEN.

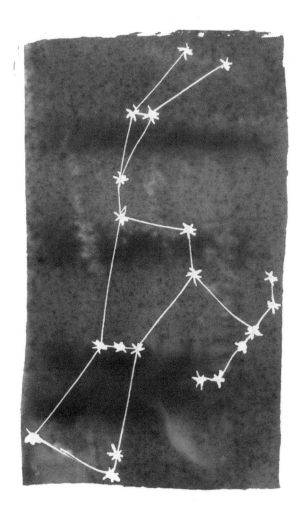

ORION

things fall apart

66 The silence that is

in the starry sky,

The sleep that is

among the lonely hills. 99

WILLIAM WORDSWORTH,
"SONG AT THE FEAST OF
BROUGHAM CASTLE"

34
FLOWERS

I've bought red geraniums for my house this year, the same as last summer. In my first summer I chose yellow chrysanthemums, but they didn't seem to like it here. Yesterday afternoon I rehomed the young plants in my window boxes, leaving compost all over my dining room table and floor. There's just the one flower in bloom so far, and I wish the other plants abundance as I tuck them into the soil.

Sometimes I wonder how much longer I'll live in this house and if it's worth investing in things like plants. But I still love looking out of my windows and seeing them there. And I think passers-by will enjoy them too, as well as any new resident who moves here next should I decide to move on.

Most afternoons I sit on my balcony, my legs under a fleecy blanket, and take in the contours of the Gelmerhörner while monitoring the blackbirds. There's something about the song of blackbird that makes it impossible for me to be unhappy at that moment. It's just so pure and innocent, verging on silly. Each time I hear them singing, I can't help but smile. I think about how the world goes on, the birds keep singing, and beauty and wonder are always there somewhere.

RED GERANIUMS IN MY WINDOW
BOXES IN SUMMER.

35
SELF-LOVE

The birds I've been watching for months go about their daily business, zipping between their trees and unleashing an unholy racket if the neighbour's cat gets too close. There's no day off for them, and they're a model of commitment to their roles as parents and providers. The trees grow around them, the flowers bloom and the bees collect and deliver. Summer has begun, singing its honest truth abundantly with the world.

I look at the world and think about my own blooming. Sometimes nature treats itself a lot better than I treat myself. I hear Iain tell me that I'm enough and I don't listen. I don't feel like I'm enough.

Lately, I am not even sure that he loves me enough. I want to hear it and feel it and see it. Even if it's my insecurity speaking, I want more. What we have now doesn't feel right. And I'm pulling away, isolating myself while nature enjoys its graceful symbiosis all around me.

36

It was a full moon last night, a pink moon. I spent the last two nights admiring it from my balcony, the lights of my house off behind me as it illuminated the sky with a backing chorus of waterfalls.

Today I decide to hike up to the Alpbachschlucht, the waterfall above Meiringen. It will be the first time I've done it this year. You can walk alongside it while clutching a thin metal cable that offers little peace of mind next to the jet of water pummelling the rocks below. This early in spring, with the path only just reopened and snow melting fast from the mountains, it's ferocious.

Not too much water builds up on the path, but I'm still not sure whether I want to walk all the way up past the waterfall at this time of year. I edge a bit higher just to see – and then higher, and higher. Otherwise I would have to walk back down to the footpath, then use the switchbacks to get to the same vantage point at Schrändli, a cluster of two or three houses at the top of the hill. About five minutes ahead of me, I get a glimpse of a local family clambering up fearlessly. So I keep going.

The best view of the waterfall is as you're walking close by it, although at the top there's a viewing platform you can walk along if you have the guts for it. It's perfectly safe, but the drop over the side of the barrier is enough to unsettle anyone. The family ahead of me were hanging out here as I started my ascent, the kids shrieking with joy and the mum telling them to calm down.

I pause for a moment to take in the crashing water below and the rock faces carved by millennia of pressure. There's a small man-made fountain up here that channels a minute fraction of the passing water, and I fill up my bottle and take a sip. It's ice cold.

THE ALPBACHSCHLUCHT WATERFALL ABOVE MEIRINGEN,
WITH A PRECARIOUS NARROW PATH ON THE LEFT.

37
DOUBTS

Three years in, my relationship has started falling apart. Slowly and imperceptibly, but surely. It shouldn't be: Iain is perfect. He's everything I should want, need and hope to have. And yet... and yet. Sometimes the most perfect people can be too right for us – they lack the drama and the uncertainty and the question marks that enthral us and leave us hanging. When you have an unrealistic and tainted view of love and yourself, something *right* is the last thing you want. And it will always feel like something is missing.

As my self-doubt has been churning, I've let my relationship dwindle – and I've started falling for someone else. We've been close friends for a while, but the boundaries of friendship are being pushed and I'm worried. He loves the mountains and we get on well, but there's no sign he will ever love me nor truly care for me in the way I need most, accepting all of my quirks and flaws and loving me just as I am. A naive part of me thinks this could change if I'm not in a relationship. An even more destructive part of me hangs on to the idea that this is what love really is: difficult and unattainable. I tell Iain that I'm worried. He tells me that it will all be okay; he believes in me and knows I'll be able to get through whatever's going on. After work, I talk to my friend Stephen. He listens, but he can't tell me what to do.

If anything can change the course of a life, it's a person you're in love with. I think of the map I'm navigating and whether I'm taking the right turn. Life looks different on both sides and I will never know which is the best decision.

I walk through the forest by the Restiturm, stopping to look over the fence of the goat meadow at the Reichenbach Falls and the mountains above. Despite everything going on inside me, nature is exactly as it should be.

38
ENDINGS

One warm Saturday evening in July, I sit with Iain on the rocky western edge of the Brienzersee. Around the corner from the swimming baths and pedalos, our feet just next to the water, I end the relationship we've spent three years building. I just want out. I need out. I need to be alone and work through the chaos swirling around in me without hurting him more. Even if it's a terrible decision, right now I know I have to make it.

39
EVENINGS

I've spent hundreds of nights here alone, most of them in silence. Or, at least, it's that real form of silence, interrupted by the small noises of life. My pen scratching on paper. The wind on the trees, a fox further down the road, yowling and disappearing into the night again. The creaking and groaning of the house. Sometimes I sit and read and immerse myself in the lives and transformations of others.

Many evenings, in the time I often talked to Iain, I stand in the shower and let the water drip over me as I close my eyes and think of nothing.

Sometimes I open wine, sliding the metal seal around the cork with my Swiss army knife. A glass for one, usually red. I sit outside on the balcony and listen to the world talk to me, passing on its wisdom and advice. Don't think about people who are no good for you. Take care of yourself like you tell others they deserve to. Prioritise your happiness.

Every night I look up at the sky and see if the stars are out. It's my favourite habit, just a small moment to check in with the cosmos and remember what I'm part of. When I'm feeling as lost as this, it buoys me. I remind myself that I'm part of the universe. That everything is changing. And things will work out – even now, when everything is crumbling into undistinguishable pieces, somehow, it will all be okay.

40
TO SET THINGS STRAIGHT

I don't claim to be anything

Other than a warm, thinking animal

Just like you

Who loves and is loved.

Don't tell me I promised more.

Don't tell me that's not enough.

41
THINGS FALL APART

The best way to fall into a pit of self-loathing: break someone's heart. For bonus points, fall in love with someone else who can never be yours. It's easy to make someone despise you, but no matter how hard you try, you can never make them love you. Sometimes the best you can do is walk away as gracefully as you can, then at least they might respect you.

I'm alone. I distract myself with my projects. Write. Take thousands of photos of the view of the mountains from my dining room window – the clouds, leaves, weather patterns, light and shadows change so much, it can hardly be called the same view. I look after my plants. Stretch and do the five basic yoga moves I know I can actually do. Physical pain would be preferable to heartache – I worry how much I mean that.

The centre cannot hold and things are falling apart. How did this all happen?

I pack tea and biscuits, hike up far into the mountains and watch the yellow-billed choughs soar over the valleys. I think about what love is and what loss is and how anyone can bear either. Is this something that other people can endure, or is it always so hard?

HIKING ABOVE THE MIST ON THE 27KM STAGE
OF THE VIA ALPINA FROM URNERBODEN TO
ALTDORF ON THE VIA ALPINA.

" The moral which some people will draw will doubtless be that the inhabitants of a valley exposed to the Föhn ought not to live in wooden houses, placed carefully end to end in the direction of the wind. [...] But it may also be worth saying that the present race has only been doing what its forefathers have done for many generations, and that it has certainly not been reckless in the sense of neglecting any feasible precautions, except that of entirely rebuilding its houses. And perhaps so thinking, they may, if they are lucky enough to have superfluous funds, bestow some slight fragment of them upon the sufferers from this very catastrophe.

"THE FÖHN", DESCRIBING MEIRINGEN IN THE SATURDAY REVIEW OF POLITICS, LITERATURE, SCIENCE AND ART, VOLUME 47 (1879)

"

42

FÖHN

Legend has it that the Föhn, the southern wind that sweeps viciously through these valleys at speeds that can exceed those of a hurricane, can drive you to madness, or *Föhnkrankheit*. The science is sparse, but anecdotes are strong, and suicides, accidents and psychosis have long been rumoured to creep higher as the wind blows. Some doctors are known to postpone surgery when the Föhn is blowing. Raising temperatures fast and nicknamed the "snow-eating" wind, it turns ice to slush and puts fear in every mountaineer in the Alps.

The Föhn has a notorious reputation here in Meiringen. It caused much of the town to burn down in both 1879 and 1891, blowing fire between the wooden houses and requiring much of the town to be rebuilt. My house, like many others rebuilt since then, is made of wood nonetheless. A few miles away at Brienz West train station, a tiny stop after Brienz's main station that only the slow local train stops at, there's a sign on the corner of the idyllic little waiting room with window boxes of pink geraniums: *no smoking when the Föhn is blowing*.

When I try to walk anywhere in it, my hood up, holding down my clothes and gripping my shopping bags with the handles wound around my wrists, I can see the very real possibility of a descent into insanity.

43
MOUNTAIN THERAPY

What helps me on anxious days: shelves stacked with books written by people who found strength and saw beauty in the world. Early mornings shared with nature. Laying my palm on the chilly surface of rocks. Looking for moss. Keeping an eye on the birds for days into weeks into months. Afternoons on the balcony with a pot of tea and a blanket, my camera next to me to try and capture the birds without disturbing them. The woods. Heading out into the world completely alone, further than I could've ever imagined possible: Greenland, Svalbard, South Africa and Morocco. Watching the sun set, night fall and stars speckle the blackness. As I explore, I'm learning which wild places guide me deeper into myself; the spaces where I can drop my facades and greet the person underneath it all.

Nearly ten years ago, life looked so different. I made myself and my life as small as possible. The world terrified me, especially people, and I wanted to be invisible. To be as unnoticed and unremarkable as possible. I wasn't sure I'd ever finish my degree. I never knew I'd one day travel alone and go on adventures and move to another country. And yet, everything has changed. So much of what I could only dream about has become real.

On my first trip to the Arctic, to central and western Greenland, much of the long days I spent hiking under a sun that wouldn't set for months was passed watching the birds. I loved the little auks soaring overhead, the size of a starling and with an intricate white front and black hooded cloak. Then there are the Arctic terns, the masters of transcontinental travel. Every year, they migrate between Arctic breeding grounds and the Antarctic: the longest migration of any bird. The average annual round-trip length is about 70,900km for birds nesting in Iceland and Greenland, and even longer if they choose to nest elsewhere, seeing two summers per year and more daylight than any other creature on the planet. Something inside them knows where they have to go and when, and they listen to that call that takes them to the ends of the earth.

On my own adventures, I've learnt that you really can transform a life. You can fall into the hands of the world, let nature hold you up and carve your new reality. On the hardest days here, surrounded by nature outdoing itself with clamouring waterfalls and intricate alpine flowers, I know that my inner landscape will become beautiful again. I'm just not sure when. In the meantime, I look for the beauty outside of myself. It is always there.

SUNRISE AT THE 4,167M SUMMIT OF MOUNT TOUBKAL IN MOROCCO IN NOVEMBER 2017 ON A SPONTANEOUS SOLO TRIP DURING MY BREAKUP.

44
THE WIND AGAIN

I've spent two years living in this house now, and feel like the walls have watched everything. I wonder what their assessment would be. Maybe, Lucy Fuggle: B+. Tidy and neat, but reads too much. Too reclusive. Looks in the mirror too many times before going out. Must get better at taking out cardboard recycling.

I love my quiet days here, but I know the best place for me is beneath the trees and heading closer to the clouds. I rarely find the answers I'm searching for between my familiar four walls, least of all the right ones. Early morning starts get me out of the house before I have time to think too much and restrict my hiding inside time to small doses, or at least balance it out with long days of alpine air.

The mountains are good for many things, but they don't help me get out of my own head. Rather, I go to them to think deeper and differently. To look at life from new angles, with a backdrop of alpine flora and a pair of eagles soaring in circles above me. Nature doesn't always offer solutions, but it shows that the landscape is always changing. And that, especially now, is what I need to know.

I wonder if we ever feel like we're ready to start blooming in a way we never have before. Or if, by the time we do, we are already unravelling our petals exactly as we need to be.

45
I'M NOT SURE I
SUFFER FROM LONELINESS

But rather the time in my own head

Going around and around and around

That loneliness makes possible.

How can one spend so much time in there

And keep it well-maintained

A perfect lawn with no weeds

Just big tulips and sweet peas and trailing clematis

Easy on the eye and sweet on the nose.

Does it come with time?

THE SUMMER VIEW FROM MY BEDROOM AND
DINING ROOM.

46
WALLS

I can hear the girl who lives in the apartment below mine when she has men over. I'm not sure if she knows this. I can also hear her sometimes when they haven't been for a while. She has a mane of red dreadlocks that screams strength and self-assurance, but boy can she cry.

47
STAGE THREE OF
MASLOW'S HIERARCHY

Memories fill the crevices in the walls and live in the boxes with the crystals that I inherited with the house. I think of all the time I spent here with Iain, and I think of the more recent time with another man who could never be the person I wanted him to be, and nor I for him.

I wonder if I need to leave here to let the memories go and start afresh. But maybe I can find a way to let go of the stories and dreams, the shared lazy mornings and quiet evenings in. Nudge them away so they can float from the windows and up the chimney so they no longer hit my heart.

The wind is roaring again, as if it's trying desperately to communicate something that we're all intent to shut out.

What would you like from me?

48
MAPS

I have a few maps on my walls here, all of them of Switzerland. Two of the maps are big, over a metre wide: one of this region, demarcated as Innertkirchen after the neighbouring town, and the other of the Jungfrau region. They're Swiss Topo maps, which are exactly what good maps should be: delicately accurate, with a colour palette that any landscape painter would be proud of. I look at their blues, greens and blacks every day, as well as my hand-drawn lines across them. I add a pen line to my maps to mark each of the hikes I do in the area. The maps are both sprawling with green veins.

Up the stairs from my front door, on the landing opposite the bathroom, the map of the Jungfrau region takes up most of the wall. That's over the other side of the mountains from me, so they're not really my home mountains. But it's the birthplace of the real Alpine giants: the Jungfrau, kept company by the Mönch and Eiger. They can't help it, but they're a bit too famous for me. I look out of my window at my less celebrated mountains and tell them, hey, people don't know what they're missing.

My map of the region around my house is on the wall in my bedroom, and I look at it when I'm sitting up in bed. I find my place on the map, just under the Restiturm, and see all the wonders hiding at altitudes above me on either side of the valley. The five lakes of the Melchsee region, where I swam late this spring, the water still shockingly cold. I look at the mountains dividing into the Grimsel and Susten passes. Mountainside meadows and rocky edges that I've wandered and sat down on to look up at the sky above me, alone and with people I love enough to take on hikes.

As summer evolves, I sketch more lines on my maps to mark my hikes. There are countless stories mapped to coordinates; joy, heartbreak, loss and love. Of life, lived out beneath mountain peaks.

49
GUESTS

I wake up one night to a scurrying noise somewhere. Sometimes I can hear birds in the attic, but this time it is much closer. I switch on my bedside light and two little eyes are looking at me from across the room. I turn the light off and try to pretend I haven't seen it, tucking my duvet underneath me to keep my feet in. I might try to be big and strong, but I've always been scared of mice.

My landlady sends over an attractive, dark-haired and well-biceped Swiss man in his mid-twenties to drop by with a mousetrap. He explains that he's heading off to the mountains to climb for a few weeks, but I can call him if I need anything.

He puts a dollop of chocolate spread on the trap and lays it out in the mouse's favourite corner. I'd put money on it being decent-quality Swiss chocolate spread.

After he leaves, I sit at my kitchen counter looking straight at the mousetrap, pondering the consequences and how I would deal with the body. I get up, trigger the trap with a stick from the wood burner's pile of logs, and put the trap in the drawer. About twenty minutes, later, I see two little eyes from the corner of the wood burner, just where the murder was planned.

It takes seven trips to the woods with my newly purchased humane mouse trap in a shopping bag before I get peace in my house. All of the relocations happen between midnight and two in the morning, waking with a jolt after the trap is triggered and the mouse panics frantically at its predicament. I'm not sure if it's always the same one, but I call them all Maurice. I wonder how the other side of the story goes: breaking in to my house, skulking around in the early hours and being dropped off back in the wood to perhaps begin the adventure all over again.

50
BLOOMING AND BREAKING

Over the last few months, a word that kept coming to mind to describe how I feel is *unbuoyed*. Another is *rudderless*. But slowly, I'm finding a way to forgive myself and start navigating back to where I need to be. I can feel roots emerging to create the foundations I'd never given much thought to before. Before now, there had always been someone to prop me up and make it seem like everything was structurally sound. I didn't have to take an honest look at how things really were inside of me. But now I have no choice.

Being here alone, without a relationship, I've had to look inside for answers. I realise just how long it's been since I've had to do that. It's so easy to let someone else create an idea of who you are and pick that up and put it on without much thought at all.

With the mountains for company, I've made my baby steps towards consolidating an identity that's wholly mine. Each time I get back into the wild, I realise how much it holds for me and how I've missed it. By merging my world with nature, so much can change. As I go further and deeper, inspiration beckons, freedom sings and I can bloom more joyfully and boundlessly than ever before.

As I put the pieces of my life back together, I think how blooming can feel a lot like breaking at first. Feeling the pain and loss and despair can be exactly what's required to create something stronger from the rubble. Now that so much has crumbled, I have less to uphold and protect. I can build my life differently. I can look after myself first and listen to the whispers that have been escalating into shouts. Treat yourself gently.

Give yourself time. Don't look to others so much for affirmation. You are enough. Just as you are. I'm learning to trust the seasons of my life and know that none of them is any more valid than the others. Everything has been for something.

During my time alone, I've been ticking off more Via Alpina hikes and extending the line drawn across the map by my bathroom door. I'm not completing them in any sort of order, just choosing them one by one based on how far away the start and end points are and the distance I feel up for each weekend. Now, my second summer in, I'm more than halfway through the list: eleven days of hiking down, and seven to go. I've crossed all of the Berner Oberland and reached the French region, or Romandie, the line on my map passing from Altdorf to Engelberg, Engstlenalp, Meiringen, Grindelwald, Lauterbrunnen, Griesalp, Kandersteg, Adelboden, Lenk, Gstaad and L'Etivaz.

But it's not about the list anymore. Every time I set off and let my body lead the way, tracing my new path between the trees and up mountainsides, I feel stronger, far beyond the ache in my calf and the new curve of muscle on the back of my thighs. Each day comes with a similar rhythm that my body's finally accustomed to: begin, ascend the peak and descend. But every section of the country is unique, with its own precious balance between delicate flora and loose rock scree, harsh ravines and soft contours, and native woodland and grassy farmland.

Entering and leaving the five cantons of Uri, Obwalden, Nidwalden, Bern and Vaud, I've noticed dialects and languages change and the smallholdings of rural farmers swapped for Louis Vuitton and wealthy tourists as I reached Gstaad. I've noticed the places that call to my heart: most of all, the routes that feel most like home, those with high mountains, alpine flowers and waterfalls in the Berner Oberland.

Whether it's a twenty-mile day hike on the Via Alpina or an afternoon stroll across the mountain to Innertkirchen, every moment I spend in nature makes it easier to put the pieces of my life back together. I get a vision of where I'm heading to beyond the path; to a place where I feel enough, where I have the courage to be me. And I know I'm getting closer.

My gift to myself is gentleness and time – time to sit on the balcony, watch the mountains and head into the woods for a few hours with no real goal other than to enjoy the presence of the trees and the creatures living in harmony with them. I go to the places where I feel most like me: most often, that's towards the edges of the valley and up, a thousand metres closer to the sky.

GETTING OFF THE TRAIN AT BRIENZ ON MY WAY
HOME FROM WORK TO SIT ON THE ROCKS, READ,
ENJOY THE VIEWS, AND SWIM FOR A WHILE.

51
PEOPLE WHO KNOW
MUCH MORE THAN I DO

For escaping to a simpler, more carefree existence with nature, read Walt Whitman. For contemplating vastness – of beauty, meaning and emotion – read Leo Tolstoy. For becoming the person you know you can be, Marcus Aurelius. For learning that it's okay to watch what you thought was your personality crack into a thousand little pieces, Frank O'Hara's *Meditations in an Emergency*. For the courage to be different, Gertrude Bell's diaries. For appreciating a sunset like it's God's greatest gift when all else is lost, read Viktor Frankl.

" Climb the mountains and get their
good tidings. Nature's peace will
flow into you as sunshine flows into
trees. The winds will blow their own
freshness into you, and the storms
their energy, while cares will drop off
like autumn leaves. "

JOHN MUIR

52

ALTDORF

The valley is orange as I near the end of my hike from Altdorf to Engelberg, the mountainsides to my left and right on fire with autumn. At 29km and with 1900m of ascents and 1360m of descents, it's one of the most strenuous stages of the trail across Switzerland. In the guide to the route by Kev Reynolds, *The Swiss Alpine Pass Route – Via Alpina Route 1*, the author advises "all but the most determined of walkers" to take advantage of the transport options available or split it into two days. But today, spending more than ten hours in the mountains up and down tricky terrain is exactly what I need.

It's 12km from Altdorf to the Surenenpass, the peak of the hike standing at 2,291m after zigzagging endless switchbacks. As I reach the jagged crags separating the two sides of the mountain, ready for my descent over the ridge, I feel utterly spent. The mist that has been enveloping me all day doesn't help and the gaps in the grey clouds are fleeting. I always pause to enjoy the top of every hike, but I don't linger today. The day isn't close to done. It is another six hours of hiking from here to reach Engelberg.

Several hours on, the mist has cleared enough to show the colours of the valley blazing. I'm the only person here, walking between the mountains with my pack feeling heavy and my feet yearning for shoeless freedom. Instead of taking more photos, I keep walking, feeling the joy of my presence in my own story, my own illustration of a girl walking through the mountains as the leaves prepare to fall.

Finally, Engelberg comes into view. It's a mountain town like Meiringen, and the farm holdings, geranium-packed window boxes and big wooden cattle sheds feel instantly familiar. But the way the valley opens up from here feels completely different. It's softer and more spacious than the valley I have made a home in; here, the gentle grassy banks of the mountainside flow smoothly into the valley floor, not like the harsher feel of Meiringen's edges. As I approach the town, I admire it, but there's no feeling of home.

Checking the train times, I realise that the next departure is in five minutes. I rush towards the railway station to make the train to Lucerne, where I'll catch the connection to Meiringen, up through the Brünigpass and down steeply into the valley, drinks bottles lurching forward as the train brakes.

It's been a day spent putting one foot in front of the other, one of the simplest things in the world. And yet, as I discover today and on so many other days here, simplicity can hold the greatest pleasure and the most meaningful answers.

HIKING FROM ALTDORF
TO ENGELBERG ON
THE VIA ALPINA IN
OCTOBER 2017.

ALPENROSE

rebuilding

" Why is it that one feels so well in nature? Because it has no opinion about us. **"**

FRIEDRICH NIETZSCHE IN A
LETTER TO PAUL RÉE IN 1877,
DURING HIS STAY AT ROSENLAUI
ABOVE MEIRINGEN

53
REBUILDING

I don't mind the rainy days here. Sitting on the balcony and listening to the patter on the leaves has a charm that perfectly clear days do not. And I like getting out into the woods with my raincoat anyway. Then there are the thundery days; the thunder always seems so much louder in a mountain valley. But some days come together with graceful perfection: clear, quiet and with the natural world in harmony.

It's mid-autumn, and every weekend with good weather is an extra blessing – one that won't last as the first snows close in. Today is just a small hike, a 10km round trip from Lauterbrunnen to Mürren to spend the middle hours of the day outside and let myself think. It's a small part of a Via Alpina stage that can make the remaining hike to Griesalp easier when I get round to it next summer.

I'm also covering a few miles of the route that J.R.R. Tolkien took in 1911, aged nineteen, on foot from Interlaken to Lauterbrunnen, up to Mürren, over Kleine Scheidegg, across to Grosse Scheidegg, and down to Meiringen and along to the Grimselpass. The path is busy here, and families are enjoying one of the last sunny weekends of the year with ice cream and backpacks full of picnic food.

In Mürren, I find a post office to get a stamp for the letter I wrote the day before. Three months after I ended our relationship, Iain has been writing to me and I've been writing back. He's been thinking about all that happened to end our relationship, and so have I – on long walks, during my evenings sitting with hot chocolate on my balcony, and when I wake up and notice the mountains drifting to autumn.

I'm not sure if we'll ever get back together. I don't know if too much has been broken. But we're listening to what each other has to say. I think of how the grass is greenest where we water it; the place where we notice if it withers or blooms. But for now I must tend to the grass right here under my feet. I have to do that before anything else.

As I get back into Meiringen and open the windows of my house, I look at the trees and my window boxes still packed with pink and red geraniums that will thrive until the frost in late autumn, having had the time to build a firm home for themselves in their soil. They're my living, breathing neighbours, like the rest of the nature surrounding my home. I water them, remove the deadheads to direct their energy towards creating new life and leave them to enjoy the late-afternoon sun. No matter what, life blooms. And disaster makes for wonderful fertiliser.

WALKING FROM GRINDELWALD TO LAUTERBRUNNEN ON THE VIA ALPINA, REACHING THE END OF THE HIKE AND THE VALLEY THAT INSPIRED J.R.R. TOLKIEN.

54
WHY I READ

To not be alone. For free therapy. To learn from the fuck-ups of people who have been here and done it all already. To fall deeply into the rich pool of beauty of this world and not surface for hours. To explore and dig out parts of me that I never knew existed: yearnings for places unvisited, surges of love and feeling for characters unlike anyone I've ever known, memories surfacing that might be real or fiction. To live the beautiful hybrid existence of a life swinging on the boundary between imagination and reality.

55
FROM PASCAL

In difficult times, always keep something beautiful in your mind.

ENJOYING THE SUNSET ON THE FINAL STRETCH
OF THE VIA ALPINA STAGE FROM L'ETIVAZ TO
ROCHERS DE NAYE.

56
MORNING BIRD

Thank you for visiting.

You lifted my heart when I thought for a moment

That all was lost.

How can anything be lost

When your feathered green chest,

The dark shadows on your back

And your delicate beak

Are right here?

57
ZURICH

After four months apart, I take the train to Zurich to see Iain on a drizzly Sunday. He meets me at the end of the platform and we're not sure whether to embrace. He makes the first move and I linger a while near his chest, remembering how much has passed since this last happened. We wander around the city, past familiar streets and with a strange feeling that despite everything, things feel as they did before.

I have always loved Zurich. Bern, the capital city, has many of the ingredients of being my favourite – the heritage, clock towers, rose gardens and compactness – although there's something about it that's never clicked with me. It doesn't inspire me as other places do; I feel bored and out of place. Bern's spirit has never called to my own like Zurich's has.

If you look beyond the wealth and business suits and fancy cars, *Züri* isn't so big after all. It's a dressed-up place that actually likes kicking back, putting logs on the fire and getting cosy with a *glühwein* and something covered in cheese on a December evening.

Coming back to Zurich today for the first time in many months, I remember how easy it feels to be here. For a place without mountains beyond little Uetliberg standing at 869m, it's still one of my favourite parts of Switzerland. As Iain has always said, it balances out life in Meiringen perfectly.

At lunch over pasta and beer, he hands me a book – *A Whole Life* by Robert Seethaler. On the cover is a mountain, a backpacked hiker almost out of sight in the bottom corner. He says the book made him think of me. When I read it that weekend, the snow is falling hard outside and there's no skiing until it clears. I stay in bed, top up my cups of tea, read it, and cry at the book and how well he knows me.

Before I get my train back from Zurich, we sit in the dark by the narrow slow-flowing Limmat, facing each other and hands in the pockets of our coats. We talk for some time and share our hurt from the summer apart. Like me, he's been with someone else. It hasn't worked out. Now sitting in front of each other, with so much changed and so much still the same, we link fingertips, notice something in each other's eyes, and kiss.

58
HEATING CINNAMON BUNS
ON A COLD WINTER AFTERNOON

Five minutes of heating gently in the oven is enough for cinnamon and cardamom to fill the house. I'm getting better at making them. Each time I roll out, coat and cut enough rounds to fill up the freezer and keep baked goods on the menu for a few weeks.

As they're finishing up in the oven, I grind coffee beans, make the brew strong, pour it steaming into my cup and inhale. Unravelling the end of the cinnamon bun, I tear a piece off and dunk one end in the coffee. A wave of espresso and Nordic sugariness warms the room.

59
REMEMBERING
WHAT'S ENOUGH

I do not need you to fill me to complete me.

I am already full of the courage,

Spirit and boldness

I have spent all these years cultivating.

It would be such a shame, a gross oversight,

To forget all of that

And feel lacking.

In truth,

I've never been fuller.

If you need do anything,

Complement me.

60

LIFE

Life has bloomed. In the last few days, the sun has beamed down on the Berner Oberland and unravelled buds into leaves and flowers. Green has taken over·and padded out the bare, scrawny post-winter landscape. The birds are joyfully noisy, their song echoing as they dart between the trees. There's a roaring backdrop to their choir; I can now hear the Reichenbach Falls before I see them. From most angles, the falls are hidden behind the unruly spruce tree that towers by the summerhouse outside my bedroom window, but they're definitely there.

Crashing water is the noise of the season, the snow melting from the ski resorts and untamed mountains up high. It's so much a wall of sound that it's essentially noise pollution – an ongoing, heavy drone performance of water colliding with rock. From my balcony, I hear it most from the Reichenbach Falls, but there's also a stream trickling down from the Hasliberg mountain resort. In the year I moved here, this became spectacularly loud – the moment I opened my kitchen windows, the noise would fill the house. For some reason it never came back as dramatically this year, just briefly after heavy rainfall. But the loss is compensated by the other waterfalls in the valley.

As I walk into the town, there's water violently ricocheting down the Alpbachschlucht. And on the train towards Interlaken for work or Lucerne to get to Zurich, I watch the waterfalls tumbling high above, dropping between three layers of hills until they reach valley level. I think of Tolkien and the inspiration he found here in the Berner Oberland to craft his universe. I wonder if any other places could be closer to Rivendell than this, the rocky, leafy utopia at my doorstep surrounded by waterfalls.

THE WATERFALL OUTSIDE MY KITCHEN
WINDOW, HEAVY WITH GLACIAL MELT
FROM HASLIBERG IN LATE SPRING.

61

MOUNTAIN GOATS

I'm seeing Iain close to once a week again. It's a strange place to be: feeling like everything is just how it used to be, with old familiarities and routines and inside jokes, while everything has changed. The best response is caution, not blind romance. Falling into how things used to be is exactly what we shouldn't be doing, and we both know this. The old way didn't work, and we need to create entirely new foundations for our relationship. Things can be stronger after they're rebuilt, but they can't be the same as before they were shattered.

I'm spending a lot of time alone, and I'm distancing myself from life in my office in Interlaken. One late afternoon at work, I sit down with one of the women in my team to review her work and she tells me she'd like a different manager who's older than me and male. I don't fit the mould of who she wants and expects to work with. I've tried so hard to change shit like this in the past. But increasingly I am too tired to fight to change it. I'm not the one to do the work right now.

It's no coincidence that over the last year, my health has been falling to pieces. My skin's worse than it's ever been. I get a urinary tract infection that spreads to my kidneys and one morning I leave work just after arriving to walk myself to the hospital. I wonder how much I am gaining from my job now, when it's so clear how much I'm losing.

Each time I get back to my house, I realise what the other option is: exchanging the praise and money and colleagues for a quieter existence with work that fits around my life, not the other way around. While spring is firmly in the air and everything in nature is transforming, I make the decision I know I should've made months ago: that I can't stay in this job anymore, in an environment that hasn't been serving me well. I'm depleted and I miss having surplus creative energy to make sparks with my own ideas.

Although giving up my income worries me, financial security isn't enough to make me stay. I hand in my notice and feel instant relief. It's done. I don't have anything to go on to next, but I have a few months of financial buffer and some people have reached out to me about freelance projects. It's a big leap, but I know it's the right decision.

I just need to get through the last month of my job. On some late afternoons, I finish up my work early, change into running clothes, and head across the river to the foot of Interlaken's local mountain, Harder Kulm. It's just 1,321m at the highest point, but the view over Interlaken and across to the Jungfrau makes it worth it, as does the challenge of the climb.

The way up is hard work over uneven terrain that's horribly steep the whole way, and the alternative of a ride on the funicular is an easy choice for most visitors. The signposts recommend three hours, but when I push myself to my limit – my face the colour of beetroot, all surplus layers tied around my waist, and my lungs feeling utterly asthmatic – I can just about make it in fifty minutes. The way down is a different story, however: with my trail running shoes on, I set off fast and forget about fear, jumping over rocks and dodging tree roots to be back in the office in twenty minutes. I love everything about it: the wind in my hair, the glimpses across the valley to the Jungfrau in the distance, and the sheer recklessness of it all.

As I fall into a state of flow with my focus purely on the ground ahead of me, it all feels so easy. I know I'm not going to fall.

I travelled alone to Svalbard last year, the place where Iain went after I first met him in Norway. It's the Norwegian archipelago you see if you look between Europe and the North Pole. I joined a snowshoe hike to a local peak with a group of four others who had somehow stumbled upon that unlikely part of the world. Two were middle-aged men from London on an unexpected getaway, the other two young Italian women who were even more unlikely polar explorers, one with shoes that the snow seeped straight through and fluffy socks you'd bring to a sleepover, soon saturated and heavy with freezing water.

We stopped at the top and took her shoes off, the guide rubbing her feet to try to bring warmth back into them. I found dry socks in my pack as well as plastic bags she could put around her feet to keep the cold moisture of her shoes away from her skin. She thanked me, and said I was like a mountain goat, at home in places like this. I've been thinking back to that here, as I turn more often to the mountains and find what I need in them. It's one of the best compliments I've ever had.

62

MATURITY

Perhaps maturity comes when I finally see how forgiving I am of others and how ruthless I can be with myself. When I notice the rift between letting people walk over me and not letting myself mess up, not even once. When I see that both of these are fixed by loving myself with a gentle open-heartedness. When I understand that I, too, am a wonderfully flawed human just doing the best I can. In the corners of my mind that have been cluttered with the question marks of self-doubt for so long, space is forming and clarity and acceptance are growing shoots and new leaves, ready for spring.

MOUNTAIN ALPENROSE ABOVE KANDERSTEG.

63
MAY

Yesterday was the last day at my job in Interlaken, and I wake up to complete freedom. I have no places to be and not much to do other than a couple of freelance projects that have been passed my way. I make coffee and head to my balcony to enjoy the morning sun.

It's also my twenty-fifth birthday today, my turn of a quarter of a century. I like the poetry of that being my first day of freedom. I love the fact that I get to spend it here, in my *Traumhaus* by the mountains on such a beautiful day. I stretch my legs out on the balcony, take a sip of coffee, and savour the bliss of having nowhere else I need to be. I welcome in this pace of life for every day, letting go of my old schedules and commitments. I know this day will always be a special one.

ALPEN-ENZIAN.

64
WHAT DAYS
LOOK LIKE NOW

Life isn't so different from before. It's nearly the same, minus spending most of my time in an office with people who steal my energy from me. How I used to spend my time outside of work is now how I spend all of my time.

It's hard to differentiate my weekdays from my weekends. I set my own schedule and decide how I'll spend my day. If there's a benefit to working from an office, it's the routine: having a reason to leave your house at a set time in the morning, walk to the train station and then do the reverse at the end of the day. I lack that now. All too often I realise it's dark and I haven't been out of the house all day.

I still need to work on my routine, that's clear, as well as my discipline. The discipline I'm lacking isn't to start working, though – I can do that. It's to know when to stop working and go out and be a part of the world.

I'm using this time to educate myself in serenity. For so many years of my life I've been stuck in a constant state of fight or flight, my body always feeling like it's running from that metaphorical bear.

As the human world around me hushes to stillness and there's only the birdsong and waterfalls, I'm becoming calmer too. My tension is easing and I feel the weight moving from my shoulders.

Inside, storms that have rumbled for years are clearing and I have the space and stability to think about the questions I've been neglecting. About where I want to be. Who I want to be. When life is rushing by, it's so easy to miss the whispers of these questions or tell them to wait. But now I can only listen.

While my environment helps me rework my inner landscape, my quiet daily rituals, away from the rest of the world, remind me who I really am underneath everything that doesn't matter. I'm not religious, but I write down Psalm 122:7 on a piece of paper next to the orchid on my kitchen counter:

May there be peace within your walls and security in your citadels.

65
HEY BIRD

You're not worried about your job, right?

Paying rent, climbing the ladder, making a name for yourself...

How's that going for you?

A CITRIL FINCH IN SPRING.

66

COLLEAGUES

I'm joined at my kitchen-counter desk by my orchid and two small green palms, which sit there and try to get my attention when I haven't watered them. There's the little wooden elephant I bought in the southern tip of Sri Lanka nearly two years ago, painted blue and with beautiful patterns across his back, face and down his trunk.

At the edge of the table is the biggest of the crystals I found in the house's box of mysteries. You can find crystals deep in the mountains here, and there's a woman who sells them near the ski lift some weekends. Sometimes I wonder which properties a more spiritual crystal owner would say this one has and hope that they are positive. Perhaps my crystals encourage you to stay in your house and spend too long filling up notebooks with thoughts and dreams; that would explain a few things.

Next to the crystal is a handful of rocks I picked up on my hikes, a few of them fossils. There's also a pine cone that grabbed my attention in the forest and a moss-covered rock. I have a little metal box with carved flowers all around it, another of the house's mysteries, that I put my wishes in. I look at it sometimes and imagine them sitting in there; pieces of paper and something beyond that too.

I'm alone here, but I can always find company. I can't remember a time when solitude scared me. How could I? It's always been a retreat for me. A place to feel safe and just be me. I know that's not for everyone. But for me, I'd rather safeguard my solitude than change it.

67
CLEANSING

With every out breath
I'm letting go of the people
Who sucked my spirit.
With every in breath
I'm nourishing myself,
Becoming more of me;
More and more free.

CROCUSES EMERGING FROM THE SNOW
ON A HIKE TO GROSSE SCHEIDEGG
FROM MEIRINGEN.

68

NEAR BLÜEMLISALPHÜTTE, ABOVE KANDERSTEG

If a god lives in nature, it's surely in the deep blue hue of the *Alpen-Enzian*, or gentian – my favourite mountain flower that pokes through the loose scree in impossible places and flags down every passing hiker to stop and praise it.

It's here in the Swiss Alps that I've learnt to love the mountains. Back in England, I grew up on flat Sussex farmland where heading out for a walk with no real purpose just wasn't what we did. But here I've become a mountain girl, someone who heads out early with a pack and a thermos, putting one foot in front of the other and spending a day lost in nature and in a forest of my thoughts.

It's not always easy, though. At the start of today's hike – and almost every hike feels like this – I'm struggling and tired. Although I'm now fit and used to going on long day hikes at least once a week, my body is wondering what on earth is going on. In particular, why we're not still in bed, reading and tucking into a cinnamon bun I've heated up from the freezer.

Earlier this morning I took the cable car to skip the first, less appealing part of the hike to the Oeschinensee, a picture-perfect lake that everyone says you can't miss when you're near Kandersteg. This time you should listen to them. It's far smaller than the Brienzersee and Thunersee; just a little blue blip on the map by comparison. But that's much of why it's so breathtaking. It's a tiny blue gem embedded at 1,578m between the mountains, the rocks rising up around it to protect its perimeter, with a path along both sides and fishing boats and opportunities for swimming within it.

But rather than just sticking to the lake itself, the best views come when you head up the painful switchbacks, on the Via Alpina trail towards Griesalp that continues to Lauterbrunnen. Here on the trail, my heart rate is up, I'm huffing and puffing, and I wonder how I can possibly think I can do this. Who am I to think I can climb mountains, especially on a hot August day where I feel like I'm melting and burning at once?

I try to go more than one switchback at a time before pausing, leaning into my hiking poles with my hat pulled down and the taste of suncream and sweat drifting onto my lips. Every so often, I look back and marvel at the view behind me, the lake set into the rocks even further away each time; becoming more and more unfathomably blue. How is it even possible that the water here can be so blue?

Now, I find the energy somewhere to push through and keep going for just a bit longer. And a bit longer. My lungs and legs wake up, work out what's going on and help me out. Until I've done what seemed impossible earlier that day. This is always how it is for me in the mountains: I always get to where I need to be.

I pass by pink alpenrose and my beloved gentian and reach the thin air where mountain birds glide on the breeze for the thrill of it. At last, I'm on the approach to the Blüemlisalphütte, the mountain cabin at 2,840m above sea level where I'll be spending the night.

Before heading into the cabin, finding my bed for the night, and waiting for a surprisingly good three-course dinner with strangers who also love the mountains, I pause for a moment. I feel the world around me and breathe in its power. I always find myself standing taller as I reach a mountaintop, propped up by the earth to feel like more of me, more powerful than I could ever be at sea level. Every peak that I reach, I find something I didn't know I had inside of me until that moment. It's less about conquering the mountain and more about collaborating. Forces acting on and against. Giving persistence and receiving strength. Thank you.

WALKING BY THE OESCHINENSEE, UP TOWARDS
BLÜEMLISALPHÜTTE FOR THE NIGHT. PHOTO BY
STEFAN TSCHUMI FOR SWITZERLAND TOURISM.

BETWEEN KANDERSTEG AND GRIESALP ON THE
VIA ALPINA. PHOTO BY STEFAN TSCHUMI FOR
SWITZERLAND TOURISM.

69
CEREMONIES

I've been trying to stay away from coffee. I've done this before. I love it so much, but my body doesn't. I get jittery, my pulse races and I feel on edge. I know I need to cut down my consumption to take better care of myself. At least until I find decaf beans that actually meet my coffee snob standards.

For now, I'm having a weekly coffee ceremony. One cup, brewed however I want it. At home, that's usually as close to an espresso as I can brew in my stove pot. I turn off any music I'm listening to and clear space in the kitchen. I grind fresh beans, make it slowly, and pour it into my white and yellow cup. I sit with it in front of me and take it all in. Hello. I love you, even if you're bad for me.

70
ASKING QUESTIONS

I'm glad there aren't many people around to ask me what I want to do with my life. The people who are close enough know me well enough not to ask. I'm where I want to be for now, isn't that enough?

I sometimes think that if something tragic were to suddenly happen, there wouldn't be that sinking feeling of, fuck, this isn't it... why am I here? Other than a difficult dual desire of wanting to go to Antarctica and spend time with my loved ones (well, and try to write something important), I don't think there's much I'd do differently.

I've been living life now – my weird Fuggle™ version of it – instead of building up plans and provisions for a later that might always just elude me. I've catapulted myself off the career path that was packaged by others so neatly for me. But I'm happy.

HIKING ON THE VIA
ALPINA FROM L'ETIVAZ
TO ROCHERS DE NAYE IN
SWITZERLAND'S FRENCH-
SPEAKING WEST.

71
BE KIND

The code for living well.

WALTER
FANKHAUSER-AEBI
1930
2014

MY FAVOURITE GRAVE BY
THE MEIRINGEN CHURCH,
OFFERING A PERFECT
VIEW OF THE MOUNTAINS
FOR THOSE WHO SHARED
A LIFE WITH THEM.

72

But I'd like to invite you

From afar

To share this day with me.

To breathe in the world's pain,

Soften it,

And breathe out our kindness.

To cherish every moment,

Especially the birdsong.

73
KEEPING IN TOUCH

I haven't kept in touch with many people from my work in Interlaken, even though it's just half an hour on the train. I only let a few of them get close to me, and it's those few people who have been around my shyness and awkwardness enough to build a friendship.

I go bouldering with Ruben sometimes, and Stephen comes over occasionally or I visit him. At his house he always tries to get me high for the first time while we watch David Attenborough documentaries. Each time I decline and he eventually leaves me to passively inhale as he enjoys my share as well as his, watching the penguins leap into the water as the iceberg comes crashing down on his TV.

I am close to both of them, although I sometimes feel like I spend my time begging them for advice on my problems while they get on with their life and never need anything in return. But other than them, there are few people I can turn to.

Sometimes it pains me how much I come across as cold to people I don't let near me. I put so much value on what friendship should be that it's near-impossible for people to make the cut. But the truth is: if our conversations are empty and skate quickly away from what matters, retreating from it as dangerous territory, I'd sometimes rather not say anything at all.

I put a lot of pressure on myself as a friend, too. I want to know what lives in your heart; what enlivens you and scares you. I want to get a glimpse of what's really you behind everything else. I want to be there for you, and you for me. If you show me your heart and I show you mine, I'd do anything on this earth for you.

74
MY OLDEST FRIENDS

I feel awestruck when I look up and remind myself how old the mountains really are. I feel like I'm with a celebrity. "Oh me, I'm nobody compared to you. You've done so much and seen so much. It's an honour, really."

CROSSING THE BUNDERCHRINDEPASS AT
2385M, ON THE 16KM VIA ALPINA STAGE
FROM KANDERSTEG TO ADELBODEN.

75
NOTE TO SELF

Stop worrying about what others think of you. What do *you* think of you?

76
TRAILS

After three whole summers, I've finally finished the Via Alpina trail across my adopted homeland. In 2015, when I went on the first hike from my front door over the mountains to Grindelwald, via the Reichenbach Falls and the Grosse Scheidegg, I made the first little line on my map, less than even a centimetre long. But I kept adding to it, catching the train when I could to the next starting point for long days in the mountains.

Gradually, with weekend upon weekend, I've walked 404km across both Switzerland and Liechtenstein, stretching from Feldkirch in Austria to Montreux in French-speaking Switzerland. Over 30,000m of altitude, each one powered by the short legs I've lamented so often.

I'm so glad I've made it happen. The thought of leaving without finishing the trail felt so incomplete. As if the only way I can fathom leaving Meiringen is after having finished this long walk that first started calling out to me three summers ago.

Each time I walk past my little map of Switzerland next to my bathroom, my hand-drawn line all the way across it, I enjoy a moment of pride and strength. Now more than ever, I know I can do big things if I just keep chipping away at them. I can push myself further than I thought possible and do things I could only dream of not long before: whether that's answering a phone call without my heart rate skyrocketing, finishing my degree, travelling alone, or walking across a country.

Even starting with nothing, things compound. Slowly things all add up and make a difference, even if it feels never-ending when you're in the midst of it. Day by day and step by step, huge things can happen.

MY MAP OF SWITZERLAND WITH MY LINE
OF BLACK MARKER ACROSS THE LENGTH
OF THE VIA ALPINA, FROM FELDKIRCH IN
AUSTRIA TO MONTREUX.

AT THE 2,223M FOOPASS, THE PEAK OF MY
FINAL HIKE OF THE VIA ALPINA, WHICH
IAIN JOINED ME FOR.

SWISS PINE

stable ground

" Come forth into the light of things,

Let Nature be your teacher. **"**

WILLIAM WORDSWORTH,
"THE TABLES TURNED"

77
MOTHER EARTH

I stood with Iain on the water's edge of the Japanese port we were about to disembark from, heading towards the art island of Naoshima, and I felt fear. "What would we do if there was suddenly a tsunami?" I asked. "Well, we wouldn't do anything," Iain replied. "We couldn't do anything."

I felt the tremors of my first earthquake two weeks later, sitting in a bar on a sandy beach on Nusa Lembongan, just off Bali. After watching the sunset, I had just finished a bowl of Indian-style curry and naan and held a near-empty beer bottle in my hand.

Mid-conversation with friends of my uncle, who I was staying with, the columns of the beachside bar started swaying and the palm trees contorted to impossible angles. After such an ordinary evening, now nothing was as it should be. We looked at each other around the table, then looked to the full glasses in front of us for the clearest indication of whether we were imagining things. Water sloshed out of mine onto the table. A flowerpot fell from the wall above us, and people starting running. I followed them to the beachfront, stopping for a fraction of a second to consider whether to head towards or away from the water.

As time ticked nearly twenty slow seconds, I felt smaller than I ever have. Strangers grabbed each other and Indonesian women who'd been here for the tsunami ten years before cried into the chests of beer-bellied Englishmen. Minutes later, our phones started buzzing: 7.1 magnitude, later adjusted to 6.9, with the epicentre on nearby Lombok. Next came tsunami warnings, and everyone headed to higher ground, albeit little more than a hundred feet above sea level.

That night, I dreamt of earthquakes. I woke up at two o'clock in the morning sure that the ground was moving. Looking at my glass of water next to me, I confirmed it. An aftershock, one of several that followed in the next few days, even with some of them likely imagined.

When the ground starts moving, the only real response is terror. I craved the firm ground of Europe and I wanted my home.

78
AUTUMN

It's November, and I'm back in Meiringen. The leaves are distributed
between the trees and the floor, but there are enough still in place for
the trees to form a sea of rich auburn, orange, and specks of stubborn
green on the hill out my kitchen window. The autumn mists roll in most
mornings, enveloping the valley and sometimes passing, other times
staying until nightfall. When they finally choose to roll out, the mountains
reappear with the snow a little bit lower down their tree line than before.
I have missed you.

WALKING IN THE WOODS TOWARDS
THE RESTITURM IN AUTUMN.

MY SKIS BY MY BALCONY DOOR, NEXT TO MY
MAP OF SWITZERLAND WITH THE LINE DRAWN
OF MY VIA ALPINA HIKES ACROSS IT.

79
ALTERNATE UNIVERSES

It's late – after eleven o'clock in the evening – and the snow is falling outside. It's already piled up high on the side of the road after the snow plough's visits and looks orangey under the streetlights. The snow weighs heavily on the spruce outside my bedroom; the branches are loaded and sagging, burdened at least for the next couple hours, before gravity wins out.

It's warm and quiet inside. I've lit candles and have a pot of orange and ginger tea I'm finishing off while writing. During moments like this when I just sit and look around, I feel proud of how I've ended up here and the life I've created. Of who I have become along the way. It could've all been so different.

There are few places I'd rather be than in my Heidi ski chalet, toasty warm while watching the snow settling. Looking out to the mountains hidden deep under thick clouds, I'm happy, safe and warm. I am so thankful.

80
JUST BEING

One of the best gifts from my time in Meiringen is having time to just be.

To be me; to let myself live on my own in a Swiss mountain town by the woods and the mountains if I want to.

To do nothing all day apart from reading, making cups of tea and writing some thoughts in my notebook.

To be separate from the world for a while. To read Tolstoy again. To make soup.

To knead dough for cinnamon buns, glaze the twirled rounds with egg, bake them to golden brown and sprinkle them with sugar, the house full of cinnamon and cardamom for the rest of the day.

To do a round of my house and check up on my window boxes, plucking the dead petals from my geraniums before gently squeezing the new buds to encourage them into the world.

To sit on my yoga mat mid-afternoon, just as the sun falls straight through the window and warms my face and toes.

To enjoy coffee occasionally, with my full devoted attention.

To have a shower in the middle of the day for no real reason other than to feel warm, alive and give my body love.

To just be, quietly, simply and slowly.

That's enough.

81

ULYSSES

I fall asleep reciting Tennyson's "Ulysses" in my head. It's an old favourite. Ever since I learnt the poem about six years ago, I've visited it hundreds of times in the foggy world approaching sleep. I think of Odysseus and Telemachus. I think of Penelope at home, weaving. I think of my adventures. I read on. How dull it is to pause, to make an end, to rust unburnished, not to shine in use, as though to breathe were life!

82

BIG QUESTIONS
WE CAN'T ANSWER

I fill a flask with hot mint tea, grab my snowshoes, and head down the road to the ski lift. My plan is to get out at Reuti and snowshoe up to Mägisalp and back on a different route down, the descent the best part with wide open views across to the Wetterhorn, Wellhorn and, from this angle, the Eiger.

It's a beautiful morning for it, and it's busy. We had fresh snow yesterday and the powder will be the stuff of dreams for locals and the handful of tourists. Two middle-aged women sitting opposite me in the lift are speaking English with the rounded, drawn-out accent of the South East. Like my own, but they don't know that. I sit there invisibly as they talk.

They're looking at the mountains above my head as we emerge from the thick line of fog. The peaks are suddenly completely clear in the rich morning light.

"How can it be," one of the women says, "that some people don't believe someone made this? That there isn't a God?" She looks out of the ski lift at the snow-capped pines and zips up her jacket closer to her chin. "How could anyone think it was a happy accident?"

"A half degree more or a half degree less and we'd be dead," the other adds.

I look ahead as the stream flows under the lift, icy in the places untouched by today's sun. Life waits, getting ready to bloom, ignorant of all of us traipsing over its mountain and just doing what needs to be done.

SNOWSHOEING ABOVE THE MIST ON
HASLIBERG. GRINDELWALD IS BEHIND
THE MOUNTAINS AHEAD.

83
BACK TO BASICS

"All good things are wild and free."

HENRY DAVID THOREAU

Freedom is my most powerful currency here in the Alps, and I realise it always will be in the places where I can thrive. I can take the afternoon off when the weather is good and catch the post bus up past the Reichenbach Falls, round the precarious corners of the tight mountain roads and up to Rosenlaui, where the mountains I'm so used to looking at from a distance stand unfathomably huge. By leaving my job and reimagining my career, I created a vacuum for the most honest version of my life to flow into.

I can sit and read and drink tea and think about life and what I want to do with each new day. Do nothing and watch the world go by without thinking about productivity. Breathe deeply. Wander in the woods and touch the cold rocks and the damp moss. Marvel at how I own a healthy body. Not weigh myself down with what doesn't matter. Live lightly. Listen to the birds and collect the colours of nature in my mind. Share joy with the world and love deeply, starting with myself.

I can redefine who I really am, behind all of the layers I've been cultivating since I stopped being an imaginative, playful child. I can remember my voice, the real one that whispers deep down what I truly want to say and create in the world. I can stop caring what people I once knew will tell their parents when they ask where life has taken me. I can believe I'm enough without changing a thing or becoming smarter or prettier. Open my heart to joy and usher in its abundance. Journey freely into the corners of the world that call to me, knowing there is a place for me there.

Everything that has broken apart has turned out to be my salvation. After I dug in the ground to find and dust off the pieces I wanted to keep, I could put them back together in a better way. I could build the most honest and thrown-open and raw version of me. And bloom.

I can finally live my own life, courageously and wildly.

84

EACH TIME I GET TO
THE TOP OF A MOUNTAIN

I love being at altitude; reaching the highest point I'll be all day, week, month, or year. My lungs are glad there's no more uphill – my legs, too. My body has been utterly spent on the journey up here. But secretly, somewhere deeper beneath the surface, I could've persevered for longer. I smile at the world below the clouds and the shapes thrown by the sun. The day is just beginning.

BY THE BLÜEMLISALPHÜTTE, ON
THE VIA ALPINA STAGE BETWEEN
KANDERSTEG AND GRIESALP.

85
CLOSURE

After nearly three years in my house in Meiringen and four overall in Switzerland, I don't want to leave. But it's time to go. I can feel that deep down. Spending my early twenties here has taught me many things, not least what I want to have in my life. It's shown me how much nature matters to me. I need it close by: from the deep green of early summer months, to the clusters of flowers, thick woodland and the song of the wild birds and rustling trees.

It's here that I've forged myself, gently at times and painfully at others. I've laughed and wept and felt pain and recovered. I'm not the same person as before. I moved here younger and softer and will leave shaped by the aches and beauty of the in-between years. I've walked hundreds of miles, swum countless mornings in freezing lakes and watched the slow arrival of the person I've become.

I've come to see how much a place can support us, lift us and console us. A home can become part of us and we become part of it. I'm fortunate – and so grateful – for these wooden walls, the people I've shared this space with and everything outside of it.

86

LEAVING

There are adventures ahead and I'm not sure yet what they're going to look like. But that doesn't matter so much. There's beauty out there. And freedom, for those who will take it.

I look around at my empty *Traumhaus* and my pile of bags. I water the geraniums a final time, lock the door and push the key into the letter box. I look at the mountains that have seen so much of me in three years – and given me so much, too. I know exactly how much I'll miss them.

Before I turn the corner to cross the bridge over the stream to head towards the train station, I allow myself one last look towards the Wetterhorn and Wellhorn and the Rosenlaui glacier between them. Then, with sadness but a deep knowing that this is the right decision at the right time, I walk towards what's coming next.

87

DREAMING

Since leaving Meiringen, I've been tending to dreams of what might follow. So far, these months after getting back to the UK have been transitory ones. A month after returning, I packed my heaviest backpack in the history of my adventures to return to Greenland three years after my first visit. That trip changed so much for me: it's where I learnt to go deeper into the wild alone and found the courage for the adventures that are now a part of me.

I wanted to experience more of what I loved most about Greenland the first time – wandering under the midnight sun with no sense of time, surrounded by a wild, isolated type of nature I'd never experienced before – so I decided to spend ten days hiking the Arctic Circle Trail.

The rhythms of camping are what I love most about it. Waking up early to boil water for porridge and tea, packing up the tent and stuffing everything into my bag before setting off for the day and finding out how my feet are doing. Watching the reindeer on the hill and an Arctic hare crossing the path ahead. Pausing to look across the fjord before submerging my water bottle and drinking straight from it; completely clear and untarnished. After a day marked only by putting one foot ahead of the other, I'd look for some flat ground with a great view close to water. Then, settling down for the night, I'd take my boots off, pitch the tent, change into my one precious set of clothes for evenings and sleeping, and boil water for food. Before bed, I'd read for hours with no need for a torch, as it wouldn't get dark for months.

Now, I'm sitting in Western Mongolia in a traditional *ger*, enjoying the warmth of the wood burner in the centre of the tent that we've just lit before bedtime, when the temperature outside will soon plummet to zero. The stars outside are some of the brightest I've seen, and the whirling haze of the milky way sits above a huge tangerine-orange moon. Three weeks ago I left Moscow by train to get here with Iain. As we passed through the anonymous forests of Siberia, for days the only change was the position of the sun in the sky.

So far from Switzerland, I think of a future I've been imagining. I have a patch of land with a small wooden house with a glass front that light pours through. Upstairs, the bedroom overlooks woodland that filters the morning sun at daybreak. Downstairs, there's a place to sit and read with just a pane of glass between the cosy inside and nature. There's a simple kitchen and a warm bathroom tucked away. A stream trickles close by, clear water flowing over mossy rocks. There's birdsong to wake up to and a porch to sit and drink tea before I start writing for the day. For late afternoon, there are wild places to explore, sit and ponder.

I wonder where this space is. I'm in no rush to find it. I have faith in dreaming; it's how we can know what we're looking for and welcome it with open arms when it turns up at our door, calling our name. Whether it's wandering the Mongolian steppe, exploring the vast expanses of China next month, back in South East England, or returning to the Alps, my job is to listen for that call. By paying attention and keeping my heart open, life will make sense as I take my next step with faith and grace, the natural world by my side.

HIKING THE ARCTIC CIRCLE TRAIL IN GREENLAND
IN JULY 2019, TEN DAYS FROM KANGERLUSSUAQ
BY THE ICECAP TO SISIMIUT ON THE WEST COAST.

reading list

Some of my favourite books about wild places and life.

A Woman in Arabia: The Writings of the Queen of the Desert
Gertrude Bell, edited by Georgina Howell

Wind, Sand and Stars
Antoine de Saint-Exupéry

Mountains of the Mind: A History of a Fascination
Robert Macfarlane

Devotions: The Selected Poems of Mary Oliver
Mary Oliver

A Whole Life
Robert Seethaler

The Living Mountain
Nan Shepherd

Brave Enough
Cheryl Strayed

How to be a Good Creature: A Memoir in Thirteen Animals
Sy Montgomery

Prodigal Summer
Barbara Kingsolver

The Sun is a Compass: A 4,000-Mile Journey Into the Alaskan Wilds
Caroline Van Hemert

gratitude

If you've read this far, thank you. I always hoped I'd write a book someday, and it turned out to be this one. Will it be my best one, who knows, but I'm just glad it exists. To all of the people who helped me to make it into something real – Alana, Bethany, Louise, Clem, Collette and my first readers – thank you.

To the people of Meiringen, thank you for showing me life in a Swiss mountain town.

To the special people who shared the mountains with me, the fact that I joined you says it all.

To those of you who pulled me out of my comfort zone where I was safe yet miserable and unceasingly nervous, thank you.

To those of you who gifted me your friendship and support when I needed it most, you have my eternal gratitude.

Thank you to Beth Gibbons, Stevie Nicks and Rachel Goswell for singing to my heart.

And above all, Iain – you are the reason I came to Switzerland, the reason this book exists, and the best person I could ask to share a life with. You helped me to design my own evolution during these years, even during our time apart. You see what I lose sight of, bring me back to the best parts of myself, and never fail to have a good album to recommend for every possible situation. I love you.

references

Epigraph

Muir, John: Undated fragment from c. 1871, attributed to an autobiographical notebook in *Son of the Wilderness: The Life of John Muir* by Linnie Marsh Wolfe, page 144 (1945)

6. Moving

Murray, John: *A Hand-book for Travellers in Switzerland and the Alps of Savoy and Piedmont*, page 95 (1874)

11. Coffee

Conan Doyle, Sir Arthur: "The Final Problem", *The Strand Magazine* (1893)

13. Afternoon walks

Muir, John: *Our National Parks*, Boston and New York: Houghton, Mifflin and Company, page 56 (1901)

Watching the world

Muir, John: *The Mountains of California*, New York: The Century Co (1894)

Things fall apart
Wordsworth, William: "Song at the Feast of Brougham Castle" (1807)

42. Föhn
"The Föhn", *The Saturday Review of Politics, Literature, Science and Art*, Volume 47 (1879)

51. People who know much more than I do
Muir, John: *Our National Parks*, Boston and New York: Houghton, Mifflin and Company (1901)

Rebuilding
Nietzsche, Friedrich. *Sämtliche Briefe: Kritische Studienausgabe in 8 Beinden* ed. G. Colli and M. Montinari, Band 5, 246, 2nd half of June, 1877, Berlin: de Gruyter (1975)

83. Back to basics
Thoreau, Henry: "Walking," *The Atlantic Monthly, A Magazine of Literature, Art, and Politics*, Boston: Ticknor and Fields. IX (LVI): 657–674 (June 1862)

Stable Ground
Wordsworth, William: "The Tables Turned" (1798)